THE BRIDGE
STUDENT TEXT

VOLUME 1 — FOR B

by Randa
and Frank

Drawings by Jude Goodwin

**Published by
Devyn Press, Inc.
Louisville, Kentucky**

Printed in the United States of America.

Devyn Press, Inc.
3600 Chamberlain Lane, Suite 230
Louisville, KY 40241
1-800-274-2221

Sixth Printing

ISBN No. 0-910791-51-1

Table Of Contents

Dedications

To C.H.
—F.S.

To Mary, Devyn and Dustin.
—R.S.B.

Acknowledgments

Grateful thanks to:
Betty Mattison for her patience and typesetting skills;
Pat Houington, Tony Lipka and Henry Francis for their editorial
 assistance;
Izzy Ellis and V.B.I. for their cover photography;
also to Mary Black, Mimi Maier, Bonnie Baron Pollack and
 Debbie Quire.

The student is referred to as "he" to make the text more readable.

Introduction

We're sure that you'll be glad you are taking the time to become a bridge player! This is a truly marvelous game, played by tens of millions, with many rewards. Your effort will be well spent.

Learning bridge is like almost any other pursuit; you will get about as much out of it as you are willing to put into it. For those who master the game, the benefits are very satisfying. At the very least, you will have a lasting way of entertaining yourself and a means of making friends wherever you go. And who knows? You might even have the makings of a world champion!

This workbook is designed to help you get the most from your bridge course. In making a beginning, there are a great many new things to learn. The material from each lesson in your course is summarized here, and there are quizzes so that you can test your understanding of that material. Try to learn as much of the material here as possible, even if it means a little old-fashioned memorization. We believe that if you learn all the material presented here, you'll be ready for anybody at the bridge table!

In addition, you are encouraged to read other books and look at the bridge column in your local paper. Try to practice and play outside of class as much as possible. If you are unable to find a foursome, deal out some hands by yourself and see if you can imagine how the bidding and play might go. You cannot learn to play this game in just 25 hours of class time.

Good luck!

A Glossary for Beginning Bridge

AUCTION

The first phase of each hand of bridge, in which both partnerships may bid for the purpose of naming the trump suit and may suggest that they expect to win a certain number of tricks in the play. The auction may take several rounds of bidding and is won by the side that bids highest. It ends when three players pass in succession.

BID

A bid consists of a number and a suit (or notrump). The number is the number of tricks *more than six* you expect your side to win. The suit is one you believe might be a good trump suit for your side; this will often be a suit in which you have several cards. You may bid notrump if, in general, you have some high cards in every suit, but not great length in any suit. So, a bid of 3 ♡ is an offer to take nine tricks with hearts as trumps.

Bids have another implicit meaning; they are used to describe the strength and shape of your hand to partner. Through careful bidding, it is possible to define your hand quite accurately. Your partnership may then be able to tell how many tricks the combined hands will produce, and what suit, if any, should be trumps.

CALL

A bid, a pass, double or redouble.

CONTRACT

The number of tricks the pair that wins the auction undertakes to make.

DEAL	The distribution of the cards, 13 to each player, one at a time. To begin the game, the players usually cut the cards to see who will play as partners and who will be dealer for the first hand. Thereafter, the deal is passed around the table clockwise.
DECLARER	The player who attempts to make the contract by playing both his own cards and those in dummy to best advantage. He is the player who *first bid* the suit that became trumps or who *first bid* notrump.
DEFENDERS	The pair that opposes declarer and tries to keep him from making his contract.
DOUBLE	A call available during the auction. Most often, if you double an opposing bid, you are saying that you doubt the bid will be made. If one of your bids is doubled by the opponents, you may REDOUBLE at your turn, expressing confidence that you will make the contract anyway.
DUMMY	Declarer's partner. After the opening lead, his cards are placed on the table for all to see and are played by declarer. The term "dummy" is also applied to the dummy's hand after it is placed down. The presence of a dummy lets declarer see his resources and plan ways of making extra tricks. The skill required for good dummy play is one thing that makes bridge unique.
FOLLOWING SUIT	Whenever possible, each player must play a card of the same suit as the one that was led to the trick. If unable to

follow suit, a player may discard or play a trump if there is a trump suit.

GAME CONTRACTS	Contracts of 3 NT, 4♡ or 4♠, 5♣ or 5◇. There are bonuses in the scoring for bidding and making games. It is desirable to bid a game if possible; otherwise it is best to stop in the lowest playable contract. Thus, accuracy in the bidding becomes important.
LEAD	The first card played to a trick. The lead to the first trick is made before the dummy is placed down and is called the OPENING LEAD.
MAJOR and MINOR SUITS	Spades and hearts are the major suits. Clubs and diamonds are the minor suits.
NOTRUMP	If the play is at notrump, there is no trump suit, and only a card of the suit that is led to a trick can win that trick.
OPENING THE BIDDING	Making the first bid in the auction.
PARTNERSHIP	Bridge is played by two pairs of partners. Partners sit opposite each other. Partnership trust and cooperation are important features of the game.
PARTSCORE	Contract below the level of game.
PASS	Any player may pass at his turn in the auction. Even though he has passed once, a player may still bid whenever it is his turn.
RANK of SUITS	Spades is the highest-ranking suit, followed by hearts, diamonds and clubs.

Notrump, however, outranks all the suits. The rank of the suits is important because, in the bidding, you may outbid the opponents by offering to take the same number of tricks in a suit that ranks higher than the suit they bid. For example, if someone has bid 3 ♡, you may bid 3 ♠ (or 3 NT), but if you wish to bid clubs or diamonds, you must bid at least four.

RUBBER

A unit of scoring in bridge. Your side wins a rubber, and a substantial bonus, if you bid and make two games before the opponents. Successful partscore contracts may accumulate toward making a game.

SLAM CONTRACTS

Contracts at the six and seven levels. Small slams and grand slams, as they are called, carry a substantial bonus if they are bid and made.

SCORING

Points are scored by bidding and making contracts, or by defeating contracts the opponents bid. Also, there are bonus points for successful game and slam contracts and for winning rubbers. You will score a few extra points for making more tricks than you have bid to take, but making what you have bid is the primary goal in the play.

TRICK

One card played by each player in succession, going clockwise, make up one trick. In playing to a trick, you detach a card from your hand at your turn and place it face up in the middle of the table.

The best card played to each trick wins that trick. There are 13 tricks to be won, and the primary object of the game is to take as many tricks as possible.

TRUMPS   In the play, there is often a trump suit, determined by the bidding. A small card in the trump suit outranks any card in each of the other suits. Remember, though, that a player's first obligation is to follow suit if he can. Length in the trump suit is an asset.

VULNERABILITY   After one side has made one game toward completion of the rubber, they are said to be vulnerable. Being vulnerable offers the chance to win the rubber by making one more game, but the penalties for failing to make a contract when you are vulnerable are greater.

Orientation For The Absolute Beginner

Bridge is played by four contestants, two on each side. Partners sit opposite each other, and partnership trust and cooperation are important features of the game.

There are two phases to each hand of bridge. In the PLAY, the players on both sides try to win as many TRICKS as possible. A trick consists of one card contributed by each player in sequence. The best card played wins the trick. Players must FOLLOW SUIT in playing to a trick if possible, and with one exception, only a card of the suit led to a trick may win that trick. The exception is that one suit is usually the TRUMP suit, and *any* card in the trump suit outranks even the ace of a plain suit. A player's first duty is to follow suit, however. Some hands are played without a trump suit, at NOTRUMP.

In the BIDDING (or AUCTION), which precedes the play, the players on both sides have a chance to bid for the right to name which suit will be trumps, or to make the play at notrump. In making a bid, they mention a *strain* (a suit or notrump) and a *number* of tricks. The number of tricks is how many tricks *plus six* they expect their side to win in the play. (The tricks won by the partnership are counted together and kept together.) A bid of 3 ♠ would therefore be a promise to take nine tricks in the play, with spades as the trump suit.

In the auction, the players get a chance to CALL in turn. The dealer gets first chance, and from there the right to call passes around the table clockwise. Each player may BID or PASS at his turn. Even though a player has passed once, he may still bid at any further turn. If a bid is made, an auction begins, and any succeeding bid must be higher than the standing bid. A higher bid is one to take more tricks in *any* strain, or to take the same number of tricks in a *higher-ranking* strain.

The strains are ranked like this:

If someone has bid 3 ♡, you may bid 3 ♠ or 3 NT, but if you wish to bid diamonds or clubs, you would have to bid at least four.

When a bid is followed by three passes, the auction is over. The final bid becomes the CONTRACT, and it is up to the side that bid higher (perhaps without any opposition) to make at least as many tricks in the play as they contracted for if they are to score any points on the deal. Their opponents become the DEFENDERS and try to prevent the contract from being made. If they do so, they score points. The player who *first mentioned* the strain of the contract becomes the DECLARER. He will play not only his own cards but those of his partner, who will be DUMMY. After the OPENING LEAD, made by the defender to declarer's left, the dummy will put down his hand for all to see. Thereafter, the hand that wins each trick gains the right to lead to the next trick, until all 13 tricks have been played to.

There are two options available in the auction in addition to a bid and a pass. If the opponents reach some contract which you feel sure will fail, you may say "DOUBLE" at your turn. You may not double a contract that your partner has bid, only one bid by the opponents. If the contract is played doubled, and your opponents do "go down" (or "go set"), the points you score are increased. However, they score more points if they make the contract. If one of your contracts is doubled, you may REDOUBLE, reexpressing your confidence in making what you have bid.

Certain contracts are more desirable than others because there is a bonus attached to them in the scoring. The most common of these are GAME CONTRACTS. There are five game contracts, one for each strain:

GAME CONTRACTS

3 NT (nine tricks)
4 ♡ (ten tricks)
4 ♠ (ten tricks)
5 ♣ (eleven tricks)
5 ◊ (eleven tricks)

Less common are SLAM CONTRACTS.

A SMALL SLAM is any contract at the six level, requiring 12 tricks.
A GRAND SLAM is any contract at the seven level, requiring all 13 tricks. These are quite rare, and it is a thrill to bid and make one successfully.

QUIZ ON THE MECHANICS OF THE GAME:

1. What is the highest-ranking suit? What suit is next highest-ranking? What strain ranks the highest?
2. The play is at notrump. West leads the ♣2, North, whose hand is dummy, plays the ◊9, East plays the ♡Q, South plays the ♠J. Who wins the trick?
3. Hearts is trumps. West leads the ♠K, North, whose hand is dummy, plays the ♠A, East plays the ♡2, South plays the ♡5. Who wins the trick?
4. How many tricks do each of these bids promise to take? 2♡, 4♣, 7 NT.
5. A bid of 3 ◊ has been made. Which of the following bids would now be allowed? 3♣, 3♡, 3 NT, 5♣, 2♠, 2 NT?

6. South opened the bidding 1 NT, West passed, North raised to 2 NT, East passed, South bid 3 NT, and everyone passed. Which player is declarer?
7. Which of the following contracts are game contract? 3 ♠, 5 ♣, 4 ♡, 4NT?
8. How many tricks are required for a small slam? For a grand slam?

SOLUTIONS TO QUIZ ON THE MECHANICS OF THE GAME:

1. Spades, hearts, notrump.
2. West, since none of the other players could follow suit.
3. South, since he played the highest-ranking trump.
4. 8, 10, 13
5. 3 ♡, 3 NT, 5 ♣.
6. South, who bid notrump first.
7. 5 ♣, 4 ♡ and 4 NT are game contracts. You need only bid 3 NT to make game, but if you bid some higher number and make your bid, you still score game.
8. 12, 13.

Lesson 1

HAND EVALUATION
OPENING NOTRUMP BIDS AND RESPONSES

Accuracy in the bidding is rewarded in bridge. To bid accurately, you must know the value of your hand and how many tricks you rate to contribute in the play. A simple method of hand evaluation is the HIGH-CARD POINT COUNT. When you first pick up your hand, you count points for each of your high cards, according to this scale:

HIGH CARD POINTS
For each ace . . . . .count 4 points
For each king . . . . .count 3 points
For each queen .count 2 points
For each jack . . . . .count 1 point

Note that this POINT-COUNT scale has *nothing to do with the scoring of the game.* It is simply a way to translate your high-card strength (your main source of tricks) into an easy-to-work-with numerical value so you can easily tell how much high-card strength you have relative to the 40 points in the deck.

IMPORTANT NUMBERS TO REMEMBER:

26 POINTS in the combined hands should produce game in notrump or in a major suit.
29 POINTS is required for the 11-trick club or diamond games.
33 POINTS should give you a good chance for a small slam.
37 POINTS should give you a good chance for a grand slam.

With fewer than 26 POINTS, you will be content to play a PARTSCORE contract (one below the level of game). On many hands, of course, you will be too weak in high cards to bid at all.

QUIZ ON BASIC HAND EVALUATION:

1. How many high-card points would an "average" hand contain? How many high-card points are there in the deck?
2. How many high-card points do each of these hands contain?

(a)	♠ A654	(b)	♠ AK65	(c)	♠ KJ65
	♡ K65		♡ KJ76		♡ Q65
	◇ Q65		◇ KQ6		◇ QJ8
	♣ KJ8		♣ AJ		♣ KQ7

(d)	♠ A65	(e)	♠ J87
	♡ J87		♡ J87
	◇ 876		◇ KQ7
	♣ KJ54		♣ AKJ5

3. How many points are required for game in notrump or a major suit?
4. How many points are required for game in a minor suit?
5. How many points are required for a small slam?
6. How many points are required for a grand slam?

SOLUTIONS TO QUIZ ON BASIC HAND EVALUATION:

1. 10, 40
2. (a) 13   (b) 21   (c) 14   (d) 9   (e) 15
3. 26   5. 33
4. 29   6. 37

NOTRUMP OPENING BIDS,
PART OF OUR BIDDING SYSTEM:

There are two meanings implicit in every bid. You suggest a certain contract, but you also tell partner something about what sort of hand you hold. A knowledge of the bidding *system,* that is, the message each bid conveys, will allow you and your partner to communicate useful information in the bidding and reach the right contract on most occasions when you have the majority of the high cards.

NOTRUMP OPENING BIDS:

OPENING NOTRUMP BIDS

OPEN 1 NT with 16-18 high-card points and balanced distribution.

OPEN 2 NT with 22-24 high card points and balanced distribution.

OPEN 3 NT with 25-27 high-card points and balanced distribution.

"Balanced distribution" means your hand contains no void suit or singleton, and no more than one doubleton.

QUIZ ON NOTRUMP OPENING BIDS:

What should be your opening bid if you are dealer, with the first chance to bid, and you hold these hands?

	(a)	(b)	(c)
♠	KJ5	AK6	AJ43
♡	AK7	A54	AK
◇	KJ65	KJ43	Q654
♣	AK7	Q54	AKQ

(d) ♠ AJ6   (e) ♠ AQ
    ♡ AK54   ♡ KQ5
    ◊ AKQ4   ◊ KQ765
    ♣ KQ   ♣ AQ3

SOLUTIONS TO QUIZ ON NOTRUMP OPENING BIDS:

(a) 2 NT   (c) 2 NT   (e) 2 NT
(b) 1 NT   (d) 3 NT

QUIZ ON OPENING 1 NT:

With which of these hands would you open the bidding 1 NT?

(a) ♠ KQ4   (b) ♠ AQ76   (c) ♠ AJ7
    ♡ AJ7   ♡ AQ87   ♡ 876
    ◊ KQ54   ◊ AK7   ◊ AK54
    ♣ J76   ♣ J7   ♣ KQ7

(d) ♠ AJ7   (e) ♠ 765   (f) ♠ A
    ♡ 876   ♡ A5   ♡ K543
    ◊ A765   ◊ AQ765   ◊ AQ76
    ♣ KQJ   ♣ AQ8   ♣ K765

(g) ♠ J8   (h) ♠ A8   (i) ♠ KQ6
    ♡ A654   ♡ K7654   ♡ 876
    ◊ AKQ7   ◊ A5   ◊ AJ87
    ♣ Q65   ♣ AJ63   ♣ AQ7

(j) ♠ —
    ♡ AJ654
    ◊ AK76
    ♣ A765

SOLUTIONS TO QUIZ ON OPENING 1 NT:

a.   Yes
b.   No. Too many points.
c.   Yes
d.   No. Too few points.
e.   Yes
f.   No. Not with a singleton.
g.   Yes
h.   No. Not with two doubletons.
i.   Yes
j.   No. Not with a void suit.

RESPONDING TO A 1 NT OPENING BID:

If your partner opens 1 NT, he has described his strength and approximate hand pattern. It is up to you as responder to take the initiative. You must see that your side arrives in the proper contract. By adding your points to those your partner has shown, you can determine at what level you should play.

For example, if you know your side has about 26 points or a few more, you should make sure a game contract is reached. Also, since you know that the opening bid shows at least two cards in every suit, you can often tell whether to make one of your suits the trump suit or play at notrump.

Here are some of your options in responding to 1 NT:

RESPONSES TO A 1 NT OPENING

With 0-7 points   PASS if your hand looks good for play at notrump. But . . .

BID TWO OF A SUIT if you have an unbalanced hand with at least five cards in your suit and you want to get out of notrump.

With 8-9 points   RAISE TO 2 NT if your hand looks good for play at notrump. This bid is invitational to game.

With 10-14 points   RAISE TO 3 NT if your hand looks good for play at notrump. Or . . .

JUMP TO GAME IN A SUIT, with a suit of six or more cards.

With 15-16 points   RAISE TO 4 NT. This bid is invitational to a small slam.

With 17-18 points   RAISE TO 6 NT or JUMP TO SLAM IN A SUIT.

With 21 points   RAISE TO 7 NT.

With 10 points
or more   BID THREE OF A SUIT with a good five-card or longer suit, planning to play game (or slam) in your suit if partner raises; otherwise to play notrump.

QUIZ ON RESPONDING TO 1 NT OPENINGS, PART 1:

Your partner has opened the bidding with 1 NT. On each of these hands, figure the number of high-card points your partnership should have. What should you bid in response to your partner's opening?

(a) ♠ K65
    ♡ A54
    ◊ 654
    ♣ 8765

(b) ♠ AJ76
    ♡ K65
    ◊ 976
    ♣ Q65

(c) ♠ A76
    ♡ K765
    ◊ Q54
    ♣ 987

(d) ♠ AJ7
    ♡ K654
    ◊ A76
    ♣ Q76

(e) ♠ A76
    ♡ AK7
    ◊ KJ65
    ♣ Q65

SOLUTIONS TO QUIZ ON RESPONDING TO 1 NT OPENINGS, PART 1:

a. You have 23-25 points, so game is improbable. Notrump looks like a suitable spot, so *pass* and play in a partscore at notrump.

b. You have 26-28 points. Bid 3 NT.

c. You have 25-27 points. Game is possible, but only if partner has a maximum 1 NT opening, with closer to 18 points. Raise to 2 NT, a bid that is invitational to game. Partner can look at his hand again and make the final decision. He will bid 3 NT with 17 or 18 points, but will pass with 16.

d. You have 30-32 points. Game is certain, but slam is improbable. Raise to 3 NT.

e. You have 33-35 points! The high cards to make 12 tricks should be available, so bid 6 NT, a small slam.

QUIZ ON RESPONDING TO 1 NT OPENINGS, PART 2:

Partner has opened 1 NT. What would your response be with:

1. ♠ K543
   ♡ 765
   ◇ Q54
   ♣ 643

2. ♠ K86432
   ♡ 7
   ◇ Q54
   ♣ 643

3. ♠ 1086542
   ♡ 7
   ◇ 654
   ♣ 643

4. ♠ K54
   ♡ QJ2
   ◇ K642
   ♣ 1064

5. ♠ J65
   ♡ 54
   ◇ 1063
   ♣ AK653

6. ♠ K75
   ♡ Q75
   ◇ AJ64
   ♣ 1064

7. ♠ KQ4
   ♡ A5
   ◇ AQ53
   ♣ Q642

8. ♠ AQ6
   ♡ K75
   ◇ AQ53
   ♣ J97

9. ♠ AK2
   ♡ KJ
   ◇ AQ753
   ♣ KJ5

10. ♠ AQ9653
    ♡ 3
    ◇ K75
    ♣ 1053

11. ♠ J3
    ♡ Q2
    ◇ AK8653
    ♣ 1065

12. ♠ KQ1064
    ♡ 64
    ◇ AJ2
    ♣ 1054

SOLUTIONS TO QUIZ ON
RESPONDING TO 1 NT OPENINGS, PART 2:

1. Pass
2. 2♠
3. 2♠
4. 2 NT
5. 2 NT
6. 3 NT
7. 6 NT
8. 4 NT
9. 7 NT
10. 4♠
11. 3 NT. (You prefer this to the 11-trick game in diamonds.)
12. 3♠ (Partner will raise to 4♠ with three-card support or better, or return to 3 NT with a doubleton.)

Lesson 2

HOW TO TAKE TRICKS
MORE HAND EVALUATION

1. *With high cards;* aces, kings and other cards that the opponents cannot beat.
2. *With intermediate cards;* cards that aren't high to begin the play but become high as the cards that outrank them are played.
3. *With intermediate cards;* with a *finesse.* This is an attempt to win a trick with an intermediate card by playing that card in third position, after one of the opponents has already played. Your chances of making a trick in this way are increased.
4. *With long cards;* in establishing long suits, it may be necessary to concede tricks to the opponents (especially if the contract is in notrump). But if some suit is trumps, you may be able to establish a long suit by trumping cards in the suit.
5. *With your trumps;* extra trump tricks may be made by using the trumps in dummy or in your own hand or in both hands.

HERE ARE 5 WAYS TO PRODUCE TRICKS LIKE MAGIC.

QUIZ ON TRICK TAKING:

1. ♠ K Q J 3
   ♡ 9 5 3
   ◇ 7 6 5
   ♣ 8 7 6

   ♠ A 5
   ♡ A K 4
   ◇ A Q 8 2
   ♣ A 5 4 3

   Contract: 3 NT
   Opening lead: ♡ Q
   Plan the play.

2. ♠ A 4 3
   ♡ 5 4 3
   ◇ K J 10 9 8
   ♣ 5 4

   ♠ K 7 6
   ♡ A K 8 7
   ◇ Q
   ♣ A 8 7 6 3

   Contract: 3 NT
   Opening lead: ♠ J
   Plan the play.

3. ♠ A K Q 4 3
   ♡ K 6 5
   ◇ 5 4
   ♣ 4 3 2

   ♠ 6 5
   ♡ A 4 3
   ◇ A K 6 2
   ♣ A 8 7 6

   Contract: 3 NT
   Opening lead: ♡ Q
   Plan the play.

4. ♠ 5 4 3
   ♡ A K 4
   ◇ K J 3
   ♣ 7 6 5 4

   ♠ A K Q 7 6 2
   ♡ Q 6 5
   ◇ Q 10 5
   ♣ 2

   Contract: 4 ♠
   Opening lead: ♣ A,
   (followed by the
   ♣ K). Plan the play.

24

5. ♠ Q 9 2   6. ♠ Q 7
    ♡ 4 3   ♡ 3
    ◊ 5 4 3 2   ◊ 6 5 4 3 2
    ♣ A 7 6 5   ♣ A 8 7 6 5

    ♠ A K J 10 7   ♠ A K J 10 9 8
    ♡ A K 6 5 2   ♡ A 6 5 4
    ◊ A 7   ◊ Q 7
    ♣ 8   ♣ 2

Contract: 4 ♠   Contract: 4 ♠
Opening lead: ♣K   Opening lead: ♣K
Plan the play.   Plan the play.

7. ♠ 5 4   8. ♠ K 4 3 2
    ♡ A 6 5   ♡ 10 2
    ◊ J 10 4   ◊ A Q 3 2
    ♣ K 6 5 4 3   ♣ A 6 5

    ♠ A 2   ♠ 8 7
    ♡ K 7 3   ♡ A Q J 9 6 5
    ◊ A Q 9 5 3   ◊ 7 6
    ♣ A 9 2   ♣ K 8 3

Contact: 3 NT   Contract: 4 ♡
Opening lead: ♠Q   Opening lead: ♣Q
Plan the play.   Plan the play.

SOLUTIONS TO QUIZ ON TRICK TAKING:

1. Declarer has eight high-card tricks and must rely on the diamond finesse for his ninth. After winning the first trick, he cashes his spades, being careful to get the ace out of the way first. He then leads a diamond from dummy and plays his queen, hoping the finesse will win.

2. Declarer should establish his diamond *intermediates*. He wins the first trick with the ♠K, saving the ace as an entry, and leads the ◊Q, overtaking with dummy's king. Overtaking is essential because, if the opponents duck this trick, declarer is able to continue leading diamonds from dummy and establish the suit.

3. Declarer wins the first trick with the ♡A and plays the ♠A, ♠K, and ♠Q. If the suit splits 3-3, the long cards are good. If one opponent has four spades, declarer must concede a spade trick to establish the fifth card as a trick.

4. Declarer can trump the second high club. Next he should draw the opponents' trumps, keeping count so he will know when they have all been played. With the outstanding trumps no longer a menace, he can set up his diamond intermediates and cash his heart tricks.

5. Declarer plans to *establish his long hearts* by trumping hearts in dummy. He wins the first trick and plays the ♡A and ♡K. Then a low heart is trumped in dummy (with a high trump, just to be safe). If the six missing hearts have all been played, declarer must draw trumps so he can cash his good long cards. He will make 12 tricks. If the hearts divide 4-2, declarer plays a diamond to his ace after trumping the third heart, so he can trump a fourth heart, establishing the fifth one. He then draws trumps as before so that the established card in hearts can be safely cashed. Note that declarer does not draw trumps immediately on this hand. He must wait until dummy's trumps have been used for trumping.

6. Declarer wins the first trick and notes that he has eight high-card tricks. He gets two more by trumping two hearts in dummy. To return to his hand a second time to do this, declarer trumps a club. He then returns to his hand by trumping another club and draws trumps.

7. Declarer wins the first trick and can do no better than stake his contract on the diamond finesse. He goes to dummy and leads the ◊J, playing low from his hand. He hopes

the $\diamond$ K has been dealt to his right-hand opponent so it can be trapped with repeated finesses.

8. Declarer wins the first trick in dummy and leads the $\heartsuit$ 10, planning a finesse against the king. He intends to draw all the trumps as soon as possible and continue with finesses in spades and diamonds.

MORE ON THE VALUE OF YOUR HAND:

In evaluating your hand, count points for high-card strength according to the 4-3-2-1 scale we learned. Long suits and, under some circumstances, short suits, are *also* a potential source of tricks, however. Therefore . . .

LONG-SUIT POINTS

WHEN YOU FIRST PICK UP YOUR HAND, ADD AT LEAST ONE POINT FOR EVERY CARD OVER FOUR IN ANY SUIT. COUNT TWO POINTS FOR EVERY CARD OVER FOUR IN A VERY STRONG SUIT or IN A SUIT YOU BID AND YOUR PARTNER RAISES.

Don't forget that the point count is merely a way of translating the trick-taking power of your hand into a number that is easy to work with in the bidding. Tricks are the bottom line. In trying to figure out the worth of a long suit, you will often have to estimate the chances that your long cards will actually turn out to be tricks.

LONG-SUIT POINTS

SHORT-SUIT EVALUATION

SHORT SUITS ARE WORTH NOTHING WHEN YOU FIRST PICK UP YOUR HAND. THEY MAY BECOME VALUABLE IF PARTNER BIDS ANOTHER SUIT FOR WHICH YOU HAVE SUPPORT. COUNT POINTS FOR SHORT SUITS WHEN (AND ONLY WHEN) YOU ARE RECONSIDERING THE VALUE OF YOUR HAND AS A DUMMY FOR YOUR PARTNER TO USE IN A CONTRACT PLAYED IN HIS SUIT.

If partner bids a suit for which you have support:

SHORT-SUIT POINTS

A VOID   may be worth as much as 5 points
A SINGLETON   may be worth as much as 3 points
A DOUBLETON may be worth as much as 1 point

The better your support for partner's suit, the more your shortness in another suit is likely to be worth.

QUIZ ON HAND EVALUATION:

1. ♠ A J 5 4 3
   ♡ K 6 5 4
   ◊ 5
   ♣ K J 3

What is this hand worth when you pick it up?
If you bid your spades and partner raises?
If you bid spades and partner bids diamonds?
If you bid spades and partner bids hearts?

2. ♠ A K Q J 4 3
   ♡ —
   ◊ A 7 6 5
   ♣ 6 5 4

What is this hand worth when you pick it up?
If you bid spades and partner bids hearts?
If you bid spades and partner bids diamonds?
If you bid spades and partner bids clubs?

3. ♠ 8 6 4 3 2
   ♡ K 6 4
   ◊ A 4 2
   ♣ Q 3

What is this hand worth when you pick it up?
If partner bids hearts?
If partner bids clubs?

SOLUTIONS TO QUIZ ON HAND EVALUATION:

1. 13; 14; 13; 16
2. 18; 18; as much as 23; more than 18, but probably not
   as much as 23, since your support for partner is not as
   good as when he bids diamonds.
3. 10 (Note, however, that the fifth spade is unlikely to be
   a trick since your suit is so poor); 10 (If partner is going
   to need to use your shortness in clubs, then the ♣Q will
   probably be of no use to him); 10.

29

Lesson 3

OPENING THE BIDDING
WITH ONE OF A SUIT

When you *open the bidding*, you make the first bid in the auction. You should be willing to open if your hand is slightly better than average, because the odds favor your side having more of the high-card strength and a greater ability to take tricks than the opponents. Most of the time, your opening bid will be one of a suit.

OPEN THE BIDDING WITH MOST HANDS CONTAINING 13 HIGH-CARD POINTS. HANDS WITH 14 HIGH-CARD POINTS ARE *OBLIGATORY* OPENINGS. YOU *MAY* OPEN WITH HANDS THAT ARE ONLY SLIGHTLY BETTER THAN AVERAGE — 10-12 HIGH-CARD POINTS — IF YOU HAVE AN ESPECIALLY GOOD SUIT OR SUITS.

In deciding whether to open the bidding in a close case, consider your *Quick Trick* structure. You use Quick Tricks to measure the potential *defensive* value of your hand (an important consideration if you are thinking about getting the auction started. Remember, the opponents may exercise their right to bid). Here is a Table of Quick Tricks:

QUICK TRICKS

AK in same suit.................2	Quick Tricks
AQ in same suit 1½	Quick Tricks
A 1	Quick Trick
KQ in same suit.................1	Quick Trick
K ....½	Quick Trick

In arriving at a value for your hand, add up your Quick Tricks as well as your high-card and distributional points.

> DO NOT OPEN ANY HAND THAT IS SUB-MINIMUM IN HIGH CARDS AND CONTAINS FEWER THAN TWO QUICK TRICKS.

In choosing the suit in which you should open the bidding, rely on these simple guidelines. Think of this chart as a list of priorities. If your hand is described by the first guideline, make that bid. If not, go to the second guideline. If your hand fits that description, make that bid. If not, go to the third guideline until you reach a guideline that fits your hand.

WHICH SUIT TO OPEN

1. WITH ONE FIVE-CARD SUIT — open one of that suit.
2. WITH TWO FIVE-CARD SUITS — open the higher ranking suit. EXCEPTION — with five clubs and five spades, open 1♣.
3. WITH ONE FOUR-CARD MINOR — open one of that minor.
4. WITH TWO FOUR-CARD MINORS — open 1♣.
5. WITH THREE CLUBS — open 1♣.
6. WITH FOUR SPADES, FOUR HEARTS, THREE DIAMONDS AND TWO CLUBS — open 1◇.

WHICH DOOR DO YOU CHOOSE?

QUIZ ON OPENING THE BIDDING WITH ONE OF A SUIT:

I. How many Quick Tricks do the following hands contain?

1. ♠ Axxx
    ♡ KQxx   _3_
    ◊ Kxx
    ♣ Kx

2. ♠ xxx
    ♡ Kxxx
    ◊ QJx
    ♣ Axx

3. ♠ AQ
    ♡ AQxxx
    ◊ Kxx
    ♣ Jxx

4, ♠ AKxx
    ♡ Kx
    ◊ Qx
    ♣ KQxxx

5. ♠ AQxxx
    ♡ Ax
    ◊ xx
    ♣ AKxx

II. Which of the following hands would you judge to be worth an opening bid?

1. ♠ Qx
    ♡ QJx
    ◊ QJxx
    ♣ KQxx

2. ♠ A109xx
    ♡ AQxxx
    ◊ Qx
    ♣ x

3. ♠ AKJxxx
    ♡ Kxx
    ◊ xx
    ♣ Jx

4. ♠ x
    ♡ AQJ
    ◊ Kxxx
    ♣ Qxxxx

5. ♠ Qxx
    ♡ AJ10xxx
    ◊ Axxx
    ♣ —

III. Choose an opening bid with each of the following hands:

1. ♠ xx
    ♡ AKxxx
    ◊ Axx
    ♣ Qxx

2. ♠ Qxxxx
    ♡ AKJx
    ◊ Ax
    ♣ xx

3. ♠ AKx
    ♡ Kxx
    ◊ Kxx
    ♣ Jxxx

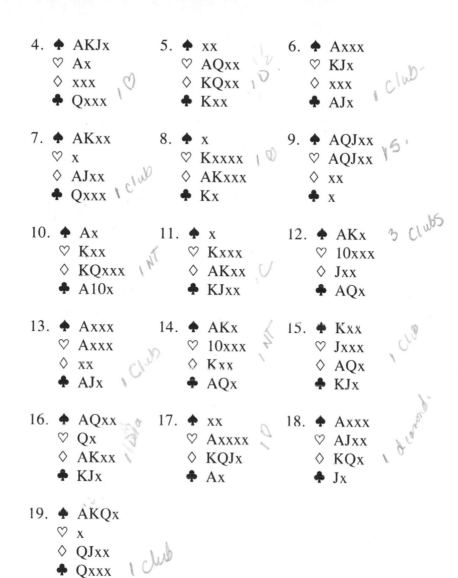

4. ♠ AKJx
   ♡ Ax
   ♢ xxx
   ♣ Qxxx   *1♡* *10*

5. ♠ xx
   ♡ AQxx
   ♢ KQxx
   ♣ Kxx   *1½* *10* *1♢*

6. ♠ Axxx
   ♡ KJx
   ♢ xxx
   ♣ AJx   *1 club*

7. ♠ AKxx
   ♡ x
   ♢ AJxx
   ♣ Qxxx   *1 club*

8. ♠ x
   ♡ Kxxxx
   ♢ AKxxx
   ♣ Kx   *10*

9. ♠ AQJxx
   ♡ AQJxx
   ♢ xx
   ♣ x   *15.*

10. ♠ Ax
    ♡ Kxx
    ♢ KQxxx
    ♣ A10x   *1NT*

11. ♠ x
    ♡ Kxxx
    ♢ AKxx
    ♣ KJxx   *1C*

12. ♠ AKx
    ♡ 10xxx
    ♢ Jxx
    ♣ AQx   *3 Clubs*

13. ♠ Axxx
    ♡ Axxx
    ♢ xx
    ♣ AJx   *1 Club*

14. ♠ AKx
    ♡ 10xxx
    ♢ Kxx
    ♣ AQx   *1NT*

15. ♠ Kxx
    ♡ Jxxx
    ♢ AQx
    ♣ KJx   *1 Club*

16. ♠ AQxx
    ♡ Qx
    ♢ AKxx
    ♣ KJx   *1NT*

17. ♠ xx
    ♡ Axxxx
    ♢ KQJx
    ♣ Ax   *1♢*

18. ♠ Axxx
    ♡ AJxx
    ♢ KQx
    ♣ Jx   *1 diamond*

19. ♠ AKQx
    ♡ x
    ♢ QJxx
    ♣ Qxxx   *1 club*

SOLUTIONS TO QUIZ ON OPENING
THE BIDDING WITH ONE OF A SUIT:

I. 1. 3
    2. 1½
    3. 3½

    4. 3½
    5. 4½

II. 1. Pass. Too few Quick Tricks to open this borderline hand.
   2. Open. Two reasonable long suits and 2½ Quick Tricks.
   3. Open. A good long suit and 2½ Quick Tricks.
   4. Pass. Very close decision. The deciding factor is that you lack length in spades, the ranking suit, and the opponents might be able to outbid you. Also, your suits are of poor quality.
   5. Open. A good long suit, plus two Quick Tricks.

III. 1. 1 ♡
   2. 1 ♠,   your *longest* suit.
   3. 1 ♣,   your *longest* suit, such as it is.
   4. 1 ♣,   no five-card suit, your only four-card minor.
   5. 1 ◇
   6. 1 ♣
   7. 1 ♣.   With two four-card minors, open 1 ♣.
   8. 1 ♡.   Open the *higher-ranking* of your two long suits.
   9. 1 ♠
   10. 1 NT
   11. 1 ♣
   12. 1 ♣.   No five-card suit or four-card minor, but three clubs.
   13. 1 ♣
   14. 1 NT
   15. 1 ♣
   16. 1 ◇.   This is a very good hand, but you must open with just one in case partner holds very little strength.
   17. 1 ♡
   18. 1 ◇   With four spades, four hearts, three diamonds and two clubs, open 1 ◇.
   19. 1 ♣

INTRODUCTION TO DEFENSIVE PLAY:
LEADING TO A TRICK

The rules of the game impose a handicap on the defending side. If you are declarer, you get to see what assets are in dummy and how they complement the values in your own hand. Often it will be clear what suits you should lead to get your tricks. But the defenders cannot see each other's hands. It can be harder to tell what course is best if you are a defender.

TO HELP OVERCOME THIS HANDICAP DE-FENDERS NORMALLY FOLLOW SOME STANDARD RULES AS THEY ROUTINELY PLAY TO EACH TRICK.

For instance, IF YOU ARE TO LEAD TO A TRICK AS A DEFENDER, and you have first picked out which suit you will lead, THE CARD YOU CHOOSE FROM THAT SUIT IS USUALLY JUST A MATTER OF STANDARD PROCEDURE. This makes defense a little easier for your side by TELLING YOUR PARTNER SOMETHING ABOUT WHAT YOU HAVE IN YOUR SUIT.

Deciding on a suit to lead often requires good judgment. A detailed discussion of suit selection will be saved until later. However, here are some rules to remember about selecting a card to lead, once you have chosen a suit:

1. If your suit contains a sequence of cards, lead the top card in your sequence. A sequence, by definition, contains *three or more cards* that are *adjacent in rank,* the top one of which must be an *honor.* However, holdings like QJ964, which contain two honors in sequence plus a third card that almost completes the series, are treated as sequences — the top card is still led.

   Sequential holdings make excellent leads and the lead from a sequence is always worth considering. It is safe and begins to establish tricks for your intermediate cards.

2. If you have a long suit headed by only two equal cards or completely full of holes, lead your *fourth-highest* card against a notrump contract, but against a suit contract consider leading the higher of your two honors.

3. From shortish suits such as J10x and KQx, lead the top card.

4. *Do not lead away from an ace against a suit contract.* Declarer may be able to trump the next time this suit is led, and you will never get the trick you deserve with your ace. If you decide to lead a suit containing an ace against a suit contract, lay down the ace first.

5. Lead the *top* card from any doubleton to get it out of partner's way. But lead low from a three-card holding.

Remember that these rules are designed to help the defenders by allowing them to tell each other something about what they have. Learn the rules on leading to a trick and use them when you play.

To summarize let us look at a chart of opening leads. Let us reemphasize that this chart tells you what *card* to lead, once you have chosen a suit.

OPENING LEADS

	Against a Suit Contract	Against a Notrump Contract
A2	A	A
A32	A	2
AK2	A	A
AK432	A	3
AQJ2	A *lead if only*	Q
AQ32	A *partner*	2
AJ102	A *has bid suit*	J
AJ32	A	2
A1092	A	10
A1032	A	2
K2	K	K
K32	2	2
KQ2	K	K
KQ32	K	2
KQ432	K	3
KJ102	J	J
KJ32	2	2
K1092	10	10
K1032	2	2
Q2	Q	Q
Q32	2	2
QJ2	Q	Q
QJ32	Q or 2	2
QJ432	Q or 3	3
Q1092	10	10
Q1032	2	2
J2	J	J
J32	2	2

J102	J	J
J1032	J or 2	2
J10432	J or 3	3
102	10	10
1032	2	2
1092	10	10
10932	10 or 2	2
109432	10 or 3	3
92	9	9

QUIZ ON LEADING TO A TRICK:

I. The opponents have arrived in a contract of 4 ♠. You have chosen to lead a heart. Choose the proper card to lead from each of these holdings.

1. ♡ Q J 10 4
2. ♡ Q J 9 4
3. ♡ Q J 7 3 2
4. ♡ Q 7 3 2
5. ♡ Q 10 8 4 3
6. ♡ J 10 9 5 3
7. ♡ J 10 8 7 4
8. ♡ J 9 8 7 4
9. ♡ K Q J 10 4
10. ♡ K Q 10 4
11. ♡ K J 3 2
12. ♡ Q 8 4
13. ♡ J 9 2
14. ♡ A 7 5

15. ♡ Q J 4
16. ♡ A 9 7 5 2
17. ♡ A K Q 6
18. ♡ J 10 5 4 2
19. ♡ K 9 8 7
20. ♡ Q 5
21. ♡ A 8
22. ♡ 10 5
23. ♡ J 9
24. ♡ K 9 6 4 2
25. ♡ 10 9 8 5 3
26. ♡ K J 10 9 4
27. ♡ A Q J 10 5

II. The opponents have bid 3 NT. You have chosen to lead a spade. Choose the proper card to lead from each of these holdings, which contain potential long card tricks:

1. ♠ Q J 10 4
2. ♠ K J 9 6 3
3. ♠ A J 6 3
4. ♠ J 10 9 5 3
5. ♠ K Q 5 2
6. ♠ J 9 8 7 3
7. ♠ Q J 6
8. ♠ Q 9 8 7
9. ♠ Q 6
10. ♠ A K Q 8 6

11. ♠ A K 9 6 2
12. ♠ K 10 9 8 4
13. ♠ Q 10 9 7 5
14. ♠ A J 10 9 4
15. ♠ A Q J 10 5
16. ♠ K Q 10 5 4
17. ♠ Q J 4 3 2
18. ♠ K 9 8 2
19. ♠ Q 8 4

III.

1. Partner has led the ♠2 against the opponents' 3 NT contract. How many spades is he likely to have? Why might it be important for you to know this?
2. Partner has led the ♡K against the opponents' 4♠ contract. Your side did not bid. What is partner likely to have in hearts?
3. Partner has led the ♠4 against the opponents' 3 NT contract. Dummy holds K83 in spades, you have Q92. How many spades is partner likely to have?
4. Partner has led the ♠6 against the opponents' 3 NT contract. Dummy holds K73 in spades, you have AJ92. What is partner's spade holding likely to be?
5. Partner has led the ♡Q against the opponents' 4♠ contract. Your heart holding is KJ964. How many hearts is partner likely to have?

SOLUTIONS TO QUIZ ON LEADING TO A TRICK:

I.
1. Q
2. Q
3. Q or 3
4. 2
5. 4
6. J
7. J
8. 7
9. K
10. K
11. 2
12. 4
13. 2
14. A
15. Q
16. A
17. A
18. J or 4
19. 7
20. Q
21. A
22. 10
23. J
24. 4
25. 10
26. J
27. A

II.
1. Q
2. 6
3. 3
4. J
5. 2
6. 7
7. Q (to get out of partner's way if he has length).
8. 7
9. Q (this would be an unusual suit to lead against a notrump contract).
10. A (hoping to take all the tricks).
11. 6 (laying down the ace and king might work well though).
12. 10 (top of an interior sequence).
13. 10 (top of a broken interior sequence).
14. J
15. Q
16. K

17. 3
18. 2
19. 4

III. 1. Four; you might want to know how many tricks might become available to your side in this suit.
2. The queen, and probably the jack (or ten) as well.
3. Four
4. Q1086
5. One or two, but no more than two. He would lead low from Qxx or Qxxx.

*OPENING LEADS ARE NOT AN EXACT SCIENCE,
BUT THERE ARE RULES TO FOLLOW.*

Lesson 4

RESPONDING TO THE OPENING BID

With 6 points or more, RESPOND if partner opens the bidding with one of a suit. You should respond, even with a poorish hand, because partner could have 20 points, or even more, for his opening, and game is still possible even if you are weak. Also, the suit partner suggests as trumps with his first bid may not be the best one available to your side. You may wish to suggest another suit. You are especially interested in finding a *major* suit for trumps if there is a fit.

While you may be obliged to respond with weakness, you may also choose to respond with a minimum bid even if your hand is fairly strong. The purpose of this is to save room in the bidding so that you and partner can exchange as much information as possible and decide on an accurate contract.

Responder's options at his first turn to bid fall into three categories:

---

1. RAISE partner's suit to two with 6-9 points and four-card support for a minor or three-card support for a major.

   RAISE partner's suit to three with 13-15 points and four-card support or better. This bid is forcing. Partner must continue at least to game.

   RAISE partner's suit straight to game with excellent support and a distributional hand, but with fewer than 10 high-card points. This bid is primarily preemptive, intended to keep the opponents from bidding.

---

2. BID A NEW SUIT at the one level with 6 points or more.

   BID A NEW SUIT at the two level with 10 points or more. Responder may bid any suit of four or more cards to suggest a suit as trumps. Any new suit bid by responder is *forcing,* and you may respond as cheaply as possible even with a sound hand in order to conserve bidding space. Therefore . . .

   JUMP IN A NEW SUIT only with a good suit or an excellent fit for partner's suit, and a powerful hand. This is a way responder can alert his partner that a slam contract is a strong possibility.

3. BID 1 NT with 6-9 points, no support for your partner's suit, and no suit of your own that you can show at the one level.

   BID 2 NT with 13-15 points, balanced pattern and a "stopper" in all the other suits. This bid is *forcing.*

   BID 3 NT with 16-18 points and balanced pattern.

QUIZ ON RESPONDING TO THE OPENING BID:

1. Partner has opened 1♠. What do you respond with:

1.	♠ Jxxx	2.	♠ Kxxx	3.	♠ Jxx
	♡ Qxx		♡ Axx		♡ xx
	◊ Jxx		◊ xx		◊ AQxxx
	♣ xxx		♣ Jxxx		♣ xxx

4.	♠ KQxx	5.	♠ AQxxx	6.	♠ xx
	♡ xx		♡ —		♡ AKxxx
	◊ AQxx		◊ xxx		◊ xx
	♣ Kxx		♣ J10xxx		♣ Jxxx

43

7. ♠ AK
   ♡ xx
   ◇ Qxxxx
   ♣ Qxxx

8. ♠ x
   ♡ Qxx
   ◇ Qxxxxx
   ♣ Kxx

9. ♠ xx
   ♡ A10x
   ◇ KJxx
   ♣ AQxx

10. ♠ Kxx
    ♡ QJx
    ◇ A10xx
    ♣ AQx

II. Partner has opened 1♣. What do you respond with:

1. ♠ Axx
   ♡ xx
   ◇ xxxx
   ♣ KJxx

2. ♠ xx
   ♡ Jxx
   ◇ Qxxxx
   ♣ Axx

3. ♠ Axx
   ♡ xx
   ◇ Axx
   ♣ KQxxx

4. ♠ xxx
   ♡ KJxx
   ◇ xxx
   ♣ Qxx

5. ♠ Kxxxx
   ♡ AQxx
   ◇ Jx
   ♣ xx

6. ♠ Kxxx
   ♡ Qxxx
   ◇ Axx
   ♣ xx

7. ♠ AJxxx
   ♡ Kxxxx
   ◇ xx
   ♣ x

8. ♠ AKxx
   ♡ Kxxxx
   ◇ xx
   ♣ Ax

9. ♠ xxx
   ♡ Kxxx
   ◇ xx
   ♣ AQxx

10. ♠ AQx
    ♡ KJxx
    ◇ xxx
    ♣ Kxx

11. ♠ AQx
    ♡ Kxx
    ◇ K10xx
    ♣ Qxx

12. ♠ xx
    ♡ AKJxx
    ◇ Ax
    ♣ KQxx

III. With each of these hands, give the correct response to an opening bid in each of the four suits.

1. ♠ x
   ♡ Q10xxxx
   ◇ Kxx
   ♣ Qxx

2. ♠ xx
   ♡ AQxx
   ◇ KJxx
   ♣ K10x

3. ♠ xx
   ♡ AKxx
   ◇ xxx
   ♣ AQxx

4. ♠ Ax
   ♡ Qxxx
   ◇ xxx
   ♣ KQxx

5. ♠ AQ
   ♡ Jxxx
   ◇ Jxxx
   ♣ xxx

SOLUTION TO QUIZ ON
RESPONDING TO THE OPENING BID:

I.   1. Pass
     2, 2♠.
     3. 2♠.   Raise partner's major whenever possible to establish the major suit fit. You aren't strong enough to bid 2◇ anyway.
     4. 3♠
     5. 4♠
     6. 1 NT. Not strong enough to bid 2♡.
     7. 2◇
     8. 1 NT. No choice.
     9. 2 NT
    10. 3 NT

II. 1. 2♣
     2. 1◇
     3. 3♣
     4. 1♡
     5. 1♠,   your longest suit.

45

6. 1♡. With two four-card majors, bid the lower. If partner has four-card support for your suit, he will raise. If, instead, he has four spades, he will bid 1♠ and you will raise.

7. 1♠. Bid the higher ranking of two long suits, both of which you plan to bid, just as in opening the bidding.

8. 1♡. Good hand, but you can afford to go slow.

9. 1♡ Show the major suit. Finding a fit in a major suit is your first goal because you score more points if playing with a major suit as trumps. Also, game at a major suit is available for only ten tricks.

10. 1♡

11. 2 NT

12. 2♡

III. 1. 1♣ - 1♡   2. 1♣ - 1♡*   3. 1♣ - 1♡
        1◊ - 1♡   1◊ - 1♡   1◊ - 1♡
        1♡ - 4♡   1♡ - 3♡   1♡ - 3♡
        1♠ - 1 NT   1♠ - 2 NT   1♠ - 2♣

    4. 1♣ - 1♡   5. 1♣ - 1♡*
        1◊ - 1♡   1◊ - 1♡
        1♡ - 2♣**   1♡ - 2♡
        1♠ - 2♣   1♠ - 1 NT

 * When you respond to a 1♣ opening bid with four diamonds and four hearts, bid 1♡ to try to immediately locate an eight-card fit in the major suit.

** You cannot raise hearts because no immediate raise shows your point count accurately. 2♡ shows 6-9, 3♡ shows 13-15. So you must *temporize* with 2♣ (a new suit bid at the two level, which shows at least 10 points), and raise hearts at your next turn.

46

INTRODUCTION TO DEFENSIVE PLAY:
SECOND HAND PLAY

As a defender, you will usually play a low card if you are second to follow to the trick. By doing so, you may:

---

(1) Make declarer guess what to play from his own hand or from dummy in third seat.

(2) Force declarer to spend one of his high cards to keep your partner (who, remember, is last to play) from winning the trick with a low card.

(3) Avoid wasting one of your high cards and one of your partner's on the same tricks.

(4) Make it more difficult for declarer to establish the tricks he needs.

There will be times you will break this rule of Second Hand Low. For instance, you sometimes can win a trick with a high card without hurting the defense. Sometimes you can prevent declarer from winning a cheap trick at no cost to your side. However, as a general rule, it will pay to be passive as second hand and wait to see what happens.

QUIZ ON SECOND-HAND PLAY:

1.   7 5 3

                                    You
                                    K J 9 2

Declarer leads this suit from dummy. Which card do you play?

2.   K 10
            You
            Q J 9 8

Declarer leads low toward dummy. Which card do you play?

3. K 7 5 2

You

A Q J 8

Declarer leads low toward dummy. Which card do you play?

4. Q 10 3

You

A J 5

Declarer leads low from dummy. Which card do you play?

5. A 7 5'

You

K 8 2

Declarer plays the ace and then leads low from dummy. Which card do you play?

6. A J 8

You

K Q 4

Declarer leads low toward dummy. Which card do you play?

SOLUTIONS TO QUIZ ON SECOND-HAND PLAY:

1. Play the deuce. If declarer has the AQ10 and he is about to finesse his ten, there is nothing you can do about it. You have no reason to do anything but wait.
2. Play the jack, just in case declarer is thinking about playing the ten from dummy.
3. Play the ace. You won't help declarer any by going ahead and winning this trick (since you have all the other intermediates in this suit). And there is a danger that you won't get your ace if you don't take it now — declarer could have a singleton.

4. Play the five. If declarer has, say, K9xx, you will help him by playing either the jack or ace. Play low and you may take tricks with both your jack and ace.

5. Play low. Declarer has Q10xx. He will have to guess whether to play his queen or his ten. In a situation like this, where declarer may be faced with a guess, you must make up your mind to play low in second seat ahead of time, so that when the crucial moment arrives, you can follow without thinking about it. If you do this, declarer won't be able to tell that you have the king and could have won the trick if you wanted to.

6. Play the four, unless you want to make sure that your side gets *one* trick, in which case you would "split your honors." If you play low, declarer might play the eight from dummy (it would be his correct play if he had 10xx or 9xx), and your partner will win a surprise trick with his nine or ten.

Lesson 5

OPENER'S REBID

OPENER'S REBID — after an opening suit bid and a response:

There are several options:

CASE ONE — If responder has made a bid that limits his strength:

PASS	if you know that no game contract is possible and you are satisfied with the contract.
IMPROVE THE CONTRACT	if partner responds 1 NT and your hand is unsuitable for notrump.
TRY FOR GAME	if responder has limited his hand in some way and there may be a game depending on whether he is in the minimium or maximum range for his bid.
FORCE TO GAME	by jumping in a new suit.
BID GAME	if you know the values for game are present and which game contract is best.

CASE TWO — If responder bids a new suit: opener must describe his hand further —

KEEP YOUR EAR OPEN FOR OPENER'S REBID.

50

RAISE PARTNER'S SUIT ONE LEVEL — with 13-15 points and four-card support (rarely, three-card support).

RAISE PARTNER'S SUIT TWO LEVELS — with 16-18 points and four-card support.

RAISE PARTNER'S SUIT TO GAME — with 19 or more points and four-card support.

REBID THE MINIMUM NUMBER OF NOTRUMP — with 13-15 high-card points and balanced pattern. This bid denies another suit you can show at the one level or four-card support for the suit your partner showed.

JUMP ONE LEVEL IN NOTRUMP — with 19-20 high-card points and balanced pattern.

JUMP TO 3 NT — with 21 high-card points and balanced pattern.

If you hold a second suit of four or more cards —

BID YOUR SECOND SUIT — as cheaply as possible with 13-18 points.

JUMP IN YOUR SECOND SUIT — with 19 points or more. This bid, a jump shift, is forcing to game.

If you hold just one long suit —

REBID YOUR LONG SUIT — as cheaply as possible with 13-15 points.

JUMP IN YOUR LONG SUIT — with 16-18 points and a good six or seven-card suit.

In theory, you may REBID any suit of five or more cards. Avoid rebidding a suit of only five cards, however, if there is an alternative. Rebid in notrump if your hand is balanced or show another suit if you have one.

QUIZ ON OPENER'S REBID:

I. You open 1 ♡, partner responds 1 ♠. What do you rebid with:

1. ♠ Qx
   ♡ AQxxx
   ◇ Kxx
   ♣ QJx

2. ♠ x
   ♡ AQxxx
   ◇ Kxxx
   ♣ AJx

3. ♠ x
   ♡ QJxxxx
   ◇ Axx
   ♣ AQx

4. ♠ Jxxx
   ♡ AKJxx
   ◇ Ax
   ♣ xx

5. ♠ Kx
   ♡ AKJxx
   ◇ A10x
   ♣ KJx

6. ♠ Ax
   ♡ AKJxx
   ◇ xx
   ♣ AKJx

7. ♠ Ax
   ♡ AKJxxx
   ◇ KQx
   ♣ xx

8. ♠ AKxx
   ♡ AKxxx
   ◇ Qx
   ♣ xx

9. ♠ Kx
   ♡ AKQxxxx
   ◇ AQ
   ♣ xx

10. ♠ AKxx
    ♡ AKxxx
    ◇ Ax
    ♣ Qx

II. You open 1 ♠, partner responds 2 ♣. What do you rebid with:

1. ♠ AKxxx
   ♡ xx
   ◇ Qxxx
   ♣ AQ

2. ♠ AKJxx
   ♡ AJxxx
   ◇ x
   ♣ xx

3. ♠ AKQxx
   ♡ xxx
   ◇ Ax
   ♣ Jxx

4. ♠ AQxxx
   ♡ QJx
   ◇ A10x
   ♣ Jx

5. ♠ AKxxx
   ♡ Ax
   ◇ xx
   ♣ Qxxx

6. ♠ AKxxx
   ♡ AKQxx
   ◇ Kx
   ♣ x

7. ♠ AQJ10xx   8. ♠ AKJxx   9. ♠ AKxxx
    ♡ Axx   ♡ KQx   ♡ Ax
    ◇ KQx   ◇ AJx   ◇ xx
    ♣ x   ♣ Jx   ♣ AQxx

10. ♠ AKQJxxx
     ♡ x
     ◇ QJx
     ♣ Qx

III. You open 1 ◇ , partner responds with 2 ◇ . What do you rebid with:

1. ♠ AKJx   2. ♠ xx   3. ♠ Ax
    ♡ xx   ♡ Ax   ♡ Qxx
    ◇ KJxx   ◇ AKJxxx   ◇ KQxxxx
    ♣ Kxx   ♣ Kxx   ♣ AJ

IV. You opened 1 ◇ , partner responds 3 ◇ . What do you rebid with:

1. ♠ Kxx   2. ♠ x   3. ♠ x
    ♡ QJx   ♡ Axx   ♡ AKx
    ◇ AJxxx   ◇ AJxxxx   ◇ KQxxxx
    ♣ Kx   ♣ Kxx   ♣ AJx

V. You open 1 ◇ , partner responds 1 NT. What do you rebid with:

1. ♠ Jx   2. ♠ x   3. ♠ x
    ♡ KJx   ♡ Axx   ♡ Axx
    ◇ AKxxx   ◇ KJxxxx   ◇ KQJxxx
    ♣ Qxx   ♣ Axx   ♣ AQx

4. ♠ Ax
   ♡ Jxx
   ◇ AKQxxx
   ♣ Qx

SOLUTIONS TO QUIZ ON OPENER'S REBID:

I.   1. 1 NT   II.   1. 2◇
      2. 2◇   2. 2♡
      3. 2♡   3. 2♠
      4. 2♠   4. 2 NT
      5. 2 NT   5. 3♣
      6. 3♣   6. 3♡
      7. 3♡   7. 3♠
      8. 3♠   8. 3 NT
      9. 4♡   9. 4♣
      10. 4♠   10. 4♠ (Solid spades, little
                                           outside strength)

III. 1. Pass   IV. 1. 3 NT   V.   1. Pass
      2. 3◇   2. 5◇   2. 2◇
      3. 3 NT   3. 6◇   3. 3◇
                                         4. 2 NT

QUIZ ON COVERING HONORS:

1.   ♡ Q x

                        ♡ K x x x

Hearts is trumps, declarer having bid and rebid the suit. Do you cover if the queen is led?

2.   ♡ J x

                        ♡ K 10 9

The contract is notrump. Do you cover if the jack is led?

3.   ♡ J 10 9 x

                       ♡ Q 8 x x

The contract is notrump. Do you cover if the jack is led?

4.   ♣ 10 9

                    ♣ K J x

The contract is notrump. If declarer leads from dummy, do you put up one of your honors?

5.   ♣ K 10 9 8

    ♠ Q x x

The contract is notrump. Declarer leads the jack from his hand. Do you cover with the queen?

6.   ◇ 10 x

                   ◇ Q x

The contract is notrump. Declarer leads the ten from dummy. Do you cover?

SOLUTIONS TO QUIZ ON COVERING HONORS:

1. No, you will make your king if you hold on to it, and there is no prospect of gain in covering.
2. Yes, you will promote your 10-9 by covering.
3. No, not with such strong intermediates in dummy.

4. Yes. This is a special case. Both you and dummy have *two* intermediates. If you cover both dummy's cards, you will promote a trick if declarer has AQxxx and partner holds 8xx.
5. No, all the intermediate cards are in dummy.
6. Yes, you might as well. Perhaps declarer has KJ8xx, leaving partner with A97x. You will gain by covering.

Remember the basis for the rule about covering honors. There must be a chance that some intermediate cards your side holds will be promoted before you "cover an honor with an honor."

BE CAREFUL WHERE YOU PLAY YOUR HONORS —
THEY ARE BIG CARDS.

Lesson 6

RESPONDER'S REBID
and
PLACING THE CONTRACT

OPENER'S REBID will often announce his strength and suggest what type hand he has, so RESPONDER, by his second turn, may have a good idea what the best contract will be. Therefore, we use the following principle for RESPONDER'S REBID:

AT RESPONDER'S SECOND TURN, HE WILL OFTEN BID TO THE LIMIT OF HIS VALUES (AS HIGH AS HE FEELS IT IS SAFE TO GO), TRYING TO PLACE THE CONTRACT OR SUGGEST A CONTRACT. DEPENDING ON THE STRENGTH OF HIS HAND, HE MAY SHOW WEAKNESS, INDICATE INTEREST IN GAME, OR BID GAME.

Here are some of responder's options at his turn to rebid. This table of options assumes that opener has not shown extra strength. If opener's rebid shows extra strength, responder needs correspondingly less strength to bid again.

PLACING THE CONTRACT.

57

WITH WEAKNESS (6-9 points)	PASS, if you are willing to play right where you are. If opener showed a second suit at the one level, RAISE to the two level with 8-9 points and four-card trump support. TAKE A PREFERENCE to partner's first suit. REBID YOUR OWN SUIT with a six-card suit or longer. BID 1 NT with a balanced hand and no four-card support for any suit bid by partner.
WITH INVITATIONAL VALUES (10-12 points)	RAISE partner's second suit to the three level with four-card support, or or RAISE his first suit if he rebids it. TAKE A JUMP PREFERENCE to partner's first suit. JUMP REBID in your own suit with a good six-card suit or longer. BID 2 NT.
WITH GAME-GOING VALUES (13 points or slightly more)	JUMP TO GAME in one of partner's suits, your own suit or notrump. BID A NEW SUIT to get more information from partner.

To repeat, if opener's rebid shows extra strength (for instance, if opener jumps in his own suit at his second turn, he shows 16-18 points and a good suit), responder may be able to bid game with as few as 8 points. A slam contract is possible if responder has an opening bid opposite opener's extra strength.

One other possible course for responder at his second turn is to ACCEPT OR REJECT A TRY FOR GAME by opener, based on whether he has a minimum or maximum hand for his previous bidding. In this auction: 1♠ - 2♠ - 3♠ - ?, responder would have to judge whether or not to go on to game, based on whether he had closer to 6 points or 9 points for his raise to 2♠.

QUIZ ON RESPONDER'S REBID:

I. *Opener*   *Responder*
    1♣   1♡
    1♠

1. ♠ x   2. ♠ xx   3. ♠ xx
   ♡ KJxx   ♡ AKxx   ♡ KQxx
   ◇ xxxx   ◇ KJxx   ◇ xxx
   ♣ Axxx   ♣ QJx   ♣ AQxx

4. ♠ AKxx   5. ♠ xx   6. ♠ Jxxx
   ♡ Jxxx   ♡ AJxx   ♡ Axxx
   ◇ xx   ◇ KJxx   ◇ Jx
   ♣ Kxx   ♣ Qxx   ♣ xxx

7. ♠ xx   8. ♠ xx   9. ♠ Ax
   ♡ KJxx   ♡ KQxxxx   ♡ AQJxxx
   ◇ KJxx   ◇ xx   ◇ xx
   ♣ xxx   ♣ Qxx   ♣ xxx

10. ♠ Ax   11. ♠ Kxxx   12. ♠ AQxx
    ♡ KQJ10xx   ♡ Axxx   ♡ AKxx
    ◇ Kxx   ◇ Jx   ◇ xx
    ♣ xx   ♣ xxx   ♣ Jxx

59

II. *Opener*   *Responder*
    1♣   1♠
    1 NT

1. ♠ AQ10xxx   2. ♠ Axxxx   3. ♠ KJxx
   ♡ xxx   ♡ x   ♡ Qxx
   ◇ Ax   ◇ xxx   ◇ AJxx
   ♣ xx   ♣ QJxx   ♣ xx

4. ♠ QJxx   5. ♠ Jxxxxx
   ♡ Axx   ♡ x
   ◇ Kx   ◇ Axxx
   ♣ Axxx   ♣ Qx

III. *Opener*   *Responder*
    1♡   1♠
    2♡

1. ♠ KJxx   2. ♠ AKxxx   3. ♠ KJxx
   ♡ x   ♡ Jxx   ♡ xx
   ◇ Axxx   ◇ Kx   ◇ AJxx
   ♣ xxxx   ♣ xxx   ♣ Qxx

4. ♠ AQxx   5. ♠ AKxx
   ♡ Qx   ♡ Qxx
   ◇ QJxx   ◇ Axxx
   ♣ KJx   ♣ xx

IV. *Opener*   *Responder*
    1◇   1♠
    2♠

1. ♠ AKxxx   2. ♠ AKxxx   3. ♠ Jxxx
   ♡ Kx   ♡ Kx   ♡ AJx
   ◇ Jxx   ◇ KJx   ◇ xxx
   ♣ xxx   ♣ xxx   ♣ KQx

V. *Opener*   *Responder*
   1 ♡   1 ♠
   3 ♡

1. ♠ KJxxx   2. ♠ AQxxx   3. ♠ KJxx
   ♡ Jx   ♡ Kx   ♡ xx
   ◊ Qx   ◊ xx   ◊ QJxx
   ♣ xxxx   ♣ xxxx   ♣ Kxx

VI. *Opener*   *Responder*
   1 ♡   1 ♠
   3 ♠

1. ♠ KJxx   2. ♠ KQxxx   3. ♠ Jxxx
   ♡ xx   ♡ xx   ♡ xx
   ◊ Qxxx   ◊ Axx   ◊ AJx
   ♣ Jxx   ♣ xxx   ♣ K10xx

VII. *Opener*   *Responder*
   1 ♡   2 ♡
   3 ♡

1. ♠ Axx   2. ♠ Axx
   ♡ Qxx   ♡ Qxx
   ◊ xxx   ◊ xx
   ♣ Jxxx   ♣ Kxxxx

SOLUTIONS TO QUIZ ON RESPONDER'S REBID:

I.   1. 2♣   (Weak)   II.   1. 3♠   (Invitational)
     2. 3 NT   (Game bid)   2. 2♣   (Weak)
     3. 3♣   (Invitational)   3. 2 NT   (Invitational)
     4. 3♠   (Invitational)   4. 3 NT   (Game bid)
     5. 2 NT   (Invitational)   5. 2♠   (Weak)
     6. Pass   (Weak)
     7. 1 NT   (Weak)
     8. 2♡   (Weak)
     9. 3♡   (Invitational)
   10. 4♡   (Game bid)
   11. 2♠   (Weak)
   12. 4♠   (Game bid)

III.   1. Pass   (Weak)   IV.   1. 3♠   (Invitational)
     2. 3♡   (Invitational)   2. 4♠   (Game bid)
     3. 2 NT   (Invitational)   3. 2 NT   (Invitational)
     4. 3 NT   (Game bid)
     5. 4♡   (Game bid)

V.   1. Pass   VI.   1. Pass
     2. 4♡   2. 4♠
     3. 3 NT   3. 3 NT

VII.   1. Pass   (Rejecting the try for game)
     2. 4♡   (Accepting the try for game)

INTRODUCTION TO DEFENSIVE PLAY: THIRD-HAND PLAY

> As a defender, you will usually play a *high* card in third seat. By sacrificing a high card, you hope to make declarer pay a price to win the trick. With one of declarer's high cards spent, your side may be able to promote some intermediate cards.
>
> There must be a chance for you to accomplish something before you put up a high card in third seat. If you can tell that your side has no intermediate cards to promote, you should not play a high card.
>
> If you have equal high cards to choose from in third seat, play the *cheapest* card among your equals.
>
> There are situations in which it is right to *finesse* in third seat as a defender, hoping to win or promote a trick without spending your very highest card.

QUIZ ON THIRD-HAND PLAY:

I. In each problem, your partner has led the ♡2 against an opposing spade contract. You must decide what to play in third seat after dummy plays low.

1.
    (Dummy)
    ♡ 7 5 3   *(Your Hand)*
♡2 led   ♡ Q 9 6

2.
    ♡ J 7 4
♡2 led   ♡ A 10 5

3.
    ♡ 9 6 4
♡ 2 led   ♡ K J 5

4.   ♡ K 6 4
   ♡ 2 led   ♡ A J 5

5.   ♡ 4 3
   ♡ 2 led   ♡ J 10 9 8 7

6.   ♡ 8 6 4
   ♡ 2 led   ♡ K Q 5

7.   ♡ Q 7 5
   ♡ 2 led   ♡ K J 10 9

8.   ♡ Q J 10 9
   ♡ 2 led   ♡ K 7 6 5 3

9.   ♡ J 7 5
   ♡ 2 led   ♡ K 10 6

10.   ♡ Q 9 5
   ♡ 2 led   ♡ K 10 8 4

II. Defending a contract of 1 NT, you lead a diamond from the ◊ K9742. Dummy has three small diamonds. Partner plays the ◊ J to trick one, and declarer wins the queen. Who has the ◊ A? Who has the ◊ 10?

III. Defending a contract of 1 NT, you lead from the ♠ K9642. Dummy has two small cards. Partner plays the ten to trick one and declarer wins the ace. Who has the jack? Who has the queen?

IV. Defending a contract of 1 NT, you lead from the ♡ J9752. Dummy has two small cards. Partner plays the king at trick one, and declarer wins the ace. Who has the queen?

SOLUTIONS TO QUIZ ON THIRD-HAND PLAY:

I. 1. Queen
    2. Ace
    3. King
    4. Jack, hoping partner has led from the queen and you can win the trick without spending your ace.
    5. Seven, the cheapest one of your equals.
    6. Queen
    7. Nine
    8. Three. With declarer known to have the ♡ A (since partner would not underlead that card against a suit contract), there is nothing to gain by playing your king.
    9. Ten, hoping partner has led from the queen.
    10. Eight, hoping partner has led from the jack.

II. Declarer has both the ◇ A and ◇ 10. Partner would always play the ace if he had it, and would play the ten if he held both jack and ten.

III. Partner has both the jack and queen, since declarer did not win the trick with one of those cards instead of his ace.

IV. Declarer has the queen. Partner would play the cheaper card if he held both the king and queen.

Lesson 7

SOME EASY WAYS TO BID YOUR SLAMS

The two main factors to consider in thinking about a possible SLAM contract are:

(1) POWER —	you need a way to produce your 12 or 13 tricks once the play gets started. Remember, about 33 points in high cards and distribution are needed for a small slam, about 37 for a grand slam. Your values may be primarily in aces and kings (at notrump) or you may have long suits and short suits to make up for what you lack in high-card strength (if the contract is in a suit).
(2) "CONTROLS"	— even a wealth of tricks will do you no good if the opponents are able to take two tricks before you get started. To make a slam, you must be able to prevent the defenders from defeating you outright — by winning two aces or an ace-king in the same suit.

SLAMS BID ON POWER — the easiest type of slam to bid is reached after a simple point-count evaluation of your strength. If your partner opens 1 NT and you have a balanced hand with 10 high-card points, you raise comfortably to 3 NT. Many slams can be bid with exactly the same ease. If you find during the auction that your side has 33 high-card points, you can bid a slam. (Note that if the opponents have only 7 high-card points, they are unlikely to have an ace-king in the same suit, so controls are no problem.)

WORRYING ABOUT CONTROLS — if you discover that your side has 33 points, *including points you add for your long suits and short suits,* you will wish to bid a slam because you have enough trick-taking power. But there is a chance that the opponents, with 8 or more high-card points, might have two aces. You can handle this difficulty by using the BLACKWOOD CONVENTION.

THE BLACKWOOD CONVENTION

A CONVENTION at bridge is a bid to which good players assign an artificial meaning. BLACKWOOD is a bid of 4 NT, used *to ask partner how many aces he holds.* He replies according to the following schedule:

With no aces	he bids 5 ♣
With 1 ace	he bids 5 ♦
With 2 aces	he bids 5 ♥
With 3 aces	he bids 5 ♠
With 4 aces	he bids 5 ♣

Note that the reply is the same with no aces *and* with all four aces. You can tell from your own hand and partner's bidding which holding he has.

If (and only if) your side has all the aces, you may ask for kings by continuing with a bid of 5 NT. Partner will reply to your question according to the following schedule:

With no kings . . . . he bids 6 ♣
With 1 king . . . . he bids 6 ◊
With 2 kings . . . . he bids 6 ♡
With 3 kings . . . . he bids 6 ♠
With 4 kings . . . . he bids 6 ♣

Whether your side can make a slam contract may depend on one or more of several factors. Note this well:

THE TIME TO USE THE BLACKWOOD CONVENTION IS WHEN YOU ARE SURE YOUR SIDE HAS ALL THE INGREDIENTS FOR A SLAM CONTRACT — POWER, EVERY SUIT UNDER CONTROL, GOOD TRUMPS — AND THE ONLY REMAINING WORRY IS WHETHER THE OPPONENTS MIGHT HAVE TWO ACES.

A player who uses Blackwood *must* be willing to make the decision about a slam bid for his partnership. Therefore, the use of Blackwood is wrong unless you are able to place the contract accurately if in possession of one piece of information — how many aces your side holds.

DON'T USE BLACKWOOD IF:

1. You aren't sure your side has the 33 points necessary to produce 12 tricks in the play.
2. You aren't sure your side has every suit under control.
3. You have a void suit in your hand. If partner has the ace of this suit, it will be of little use to you.

BE CAREFUL ABOUT USING BLACKWOOD IF:

1. Clubs is to be the trump suit. Your partner's response to 4 NT may carry you past game in clubs when game is all that can be made.

Finally . . . a bid of 4 NT can be used in TWO ways, both as a RAISE of notrump, inviting slam; and as the BLACKWOOD CONVENTION. When your side has balanced hands, you can bid accurately just on the basis of your point-count, so Blackwood is not needed. A RAISE of 1 NT to 4 NT is therefore a natural bid, inviting slam in notrump. It is when you are interested in a suit contract and may be bidding partly on the basis of good distribution that you must worry about missing high-card strength. So you may need to employ Blackwood.

QUIZ ON SLAM BIDDING:

1. How many points are required for a small slam contract?
2. How many points are required for a grand slam contract?
3. Can you add points for your short suits if the hand is to be played at notrump?
4. What are some factors that determine whether you can make a slam contract?

Partner has opened 1 NT. What do you bid with:

5. ♠ Axx   6. ♠ AQx   7. ♠ AQx
   ♡ Kxx   ♡ Kxx   ♡ Kxx
   ◇ AQxx   ◇ Kxx   ◇ AQJxx
   ♣ KJx   ♣ KJxx   ♣ AJ

8. ♠ —
   ♡ AJ10xxx
   ◇ Kxx
   ♣ AQxx

69

What would you bid in these situations?

9.   *Opener*   *Responder*   ♠ x
     1 ♦   1 ♡   ♡ AQxxx
     3 ♡   ?   ♦ Axx
                               ♣ AJxx

10. 1 ♦   3 ♦   ♠ Ax
     ?   ♡ Axx
                               ♦ AQxxxx
                               ♣ Kx

11. 1 ♠   3 ♠   ♠ AJxxx
     ?   ♡ Kxx
                               ♦ AJx
                               ♣ Ax

12. 1 ♡   1 ♠   ♠ Axxxx
     4 ♠   ?   ♡ Jx
                               ♦ Axxx
                               ♣ Kx

13. 1 ♡   1 ♠   ♠ AQxxx
     3 ♣   ?   ♡ xx
                               ♦ x
                               ♣ Axxxx

14. 1 ♣   1 ♠   ♠ AQxxx
     3 ♣   ?   ♡ x
                               ♦ AJxx
                               ♣ Qxx

What would you bid in these situations?

15. | Opener | Responder | ♠ KQJxx |
    |--------|-----------|---------|
    | 1 ♠ | 3 ♠ | ♡ Kx |
    | ? | | ◊ x |
    | | | ♣ AKJxx |

16. | 1 ♠ | 3 ♠ | ♠ KQJxx |
    |------|-----|---------|
    | 4 NT | 5 ◊ | ♡ Kx |
    | ? | | ◊ x |
    | | | ♣ AKJxx |

17. | 1 ♠ | 3 ♠ | ♠ KQJxx |
    |------|-----|---------|
    | 4 NT | 5 ♠ | ♡ Kx |
    | ? | | ◊ x |
    | | | ♣ AKJxx |

18. | 1 ♠ | 3 ♠ | ♠ KQJxx |
    |------|-----|---------|
    | 4 NT | 5 ♡ | ♡ Kx |
    | ? | | ◊ x |
    | | | ♣ AKJxx |

19. | 1 ◊ | 2 ♠ | ♠ AQJxx |
    |-----|------|---------|
    | 3 ♠ | 4 NT | ♡ Kx |
    | 5 ♡ | ? | ◊ Qxx |
    | | | ♣ AKx |

You opened 1 ♣ and partner responded 3 ♣ (13-15 points, four or more good clubs, forcing). With which of these hands would you be willing to use the Blackwood Convention?

20. ♠ —   21. ♠ AKQ   22. ♠ KJxx
    ♡ AKxx   ♡ Kxxx   ♡ Kxxx
    ◊ Kxxx   ◊ A   ◊ x
    ♣ AJxxx   ♣ Jxxxx   ♣ AKQx

23. ♠ xx   24. ♠ AKx
    ♡ AQx   ♡ AQx
    ◊ Axx   ◊ x
    ♣ Axxxx   ♣ KJxxxx

SOLUTIONS TO QUIZ ON SLAM BIDDING:

1. 33
2. 37
3. No
4. Power, every suit under control, good trumps, at least three aces.
5. 6 NT
6. 4 NT, invitational to 6 NT
7. 7 NT
8. 6♡
9. 6♡
10. 6◊
11. 5♠, invitational to slam
12. 6♠
13. 6♣
14. 6♣

In examples 5-14, one player can leap to slam (or invite) based strictly on the POWER he knows the combined hands hold, plus the assurance that every suit must be under control.

15. 4 NT, Blackwood, to check on the possibility of two missing aces.
16. 5♠
17. 7♠
18. 6♠
19. 5 NT, intending to bid a grand slam in spades if partner has the two missing kings.
20. No. DON'T USE BLACKWOOD with a void suit in your hand.

21. No. Your weak trumps are a worry that won't be solved by using Blackwood.
22. No. If partner has only one ace, you will be past 5 ♣, your only makable game. Be careful about using Blackwood when clubs is the agreed trump.
23. No. This hand is too weak to be interested in a slam.
24. Yes. This hand is fine for Blackwood.

INTRODUCTION TO DEFENSIVE PLAY: PLANNING YOUR STRATEGY

Relying on the defensive rules we have learned so far will allow you to play correctly to many tricks without giving the matter much thought. But you will meet many situations, especially when it comes to deciding what suits you should lead, that require good judgment. The defenders must keep some common STRATEGIES in mind during the play.

AGAINST NOTRUMP CONTRACTS:

1. With declarer's side usually in possession of most of the high cards, the defenders' best hope of tricks will be the establishment of a long suit. They invariably lead their longest suit and continue to lead it at every opportunity, hoping to establish the long cards before declarer can set up the tricks he needs. If you get a chance to lead, it will probably be right to RETURN A SUIT YOUR PARTNER LED TO START WITH. However . . .

2. The defenders may occasionally defer setting up their long suit while they try to prevent declarer from making use of his best suit. One way the defense may be able to accomplish this is by holding up a high card that declarer must force out to establish his suit. The defenders may be able to ruin declarer's communications.

AGAINST SUIT CONTRACTS:

1. Long cards are of no use to the defenders since declarer will be able to trump them. So the defenders try to win tricks with high cards: aces and kings that they can cash right away; intermediate cards they establish; and high cards that are worth tricks as a result of finesses won by the defense or lost by declarer.

2. Hoping to force declarer to take losing finesses, the defenders often adopt the strategy of LEADING THROUGH STRENGTH and UP TO WEAKNESS. It may be questionable strategy, however, to lead through a suit dummy or declarer is *exceptionally* strong in. It may be better to risk the lead of another suit that your side might find productive.

3. A "ruff-and-discard" occurs when the defenders lead a suit in which both declarer and dummy are void. Declarer can discard a loser from one hand while the other trumps. Since declarer may be able to avoid a loser in this way, a "ruff-sluff" often is damaging to the defense.

4. The defenders should *keep in mind how many tricks they need* to defeat the contract and then look for likely ways to get them.

DEFENSE AGAINST SUITS.

QUIZ ON PLANNING YOUR STRATEGY AS A DEFENDER:

1.

♠ A 5 3
♡ A 6
◇ 7 6 5
♣ K 8 7 6 5

♠ Q 9
♡ 10 6 5
◇ J 10 8 4 2
♣ Q 9 4

South opened 1 NT, North raised to 3 NT. Your partner, West, led the ♠6 and declarer won your queen with the king. He played the ace, king and a low club, giving up a trick to your queen. What should you lead at this point?

2.
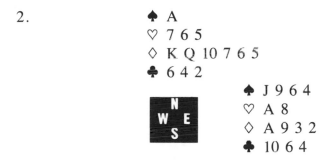

♠ A
♡ 7 6 5
◇ K Q 10 7 6 5
♣ 6 4 2

♠ J 9 6 4
♡ A 8
◇ A 9 3 2
♣ 10 6 4

South opened 1 NT, North raised to 3 NT. Your partner, West, led the ♡2 and you win the ace. What should you lead now?

3.

♠ A 5
♡ 7 5 3
◇ Q J 9 2
♣ Q J 9 8

♠ J 7 3
♡ 9 6 4
◇ 5 4 3
♣ A 7 4 2

South opened 1 NT, North raised to 3 NT. West, your partner, led the ♠6 and dummy's ace won. Declarer now led the ♣8 from dummy. What should you do here?

4.

♠ A J 2
♡ 7 4
◇ J 9 6 4 2
♣ J 10 3

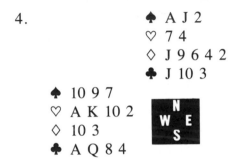

♠ 10 9 7
♡ A K 10 2
◇ 10 3
♣ A Q 8 4

South is declarer at a 3 ◇ contract. You cash the ♡A and ♡K, dropping declarer's queen. What should your next lead be?

5.

♠ 7 5
♡ 9 5 3
◇ A Q 10 3
♣ J 9 5 4

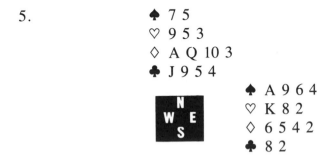

♠ A 9 6 4
♡ K 8 2
◇ 6 5 4 2
♣ 8 2

South is declarer at a 3♣ contract. Your partner, West, leads the ♠Q. How should you defend?

6.
　　　　　　　♠ K Q J
　　　　　　　♡ K 5
　　　　　　　◇ A J 4
　　　　　　　♣ A K J 9 4
　　　　　　　　　　　♠ 8 7
　　　　　　N　　　♡ A 8 6 4
　　　　W　　E　　◇ Q 10 5
　　　　　　S　　　♣ 7 6 5 3

North opened 2 NT, South responded 3 ♠, North raised to 4 ♠.
West, your partner, leads the ♡ J, and dummy's king is played.
How should you defend?

SOLUTIONS TO QUIZ ON DEFENSIVE STRATEGY:

1. Lead the ♠9, hoping to establish partner's long suit.
2. This time, partner's lead of the ♡2 suggests that he has only a four-card suit, so there are not enough tricks to establish in that suit. Switch plans and try to keep declarer from using dummy's diamonds. Return a low spade, knocking out dummy's ace, so that declarer cannot use it as an entry after establishing dummy's diamonds. Later, you plan to hold up your ◊A until declarer has no more in his hand, and dummy's suit will be left high and dry.
3. Play the ♣A and lead a spade (partner's suit). You should be delighted to have an opportunity to help establish partner's long suit. (This is a good time to make an exception to the rule "Second Hand Low.")
4. Lead the ♠10. You hope that partner has honors, which will be tricks since they will lie behind dummy's honors. This is a typical THROUGH-STRENGTH situation.
5. Win the ♠A and lead the ♡2 UP TO dummy's WEAKNESS, THROUGH whatever heart STRENGTH declarer may have.
6. Lead the ◊5. You know declarer has the ♡Q, from partner's lead of the jack, so even if partner has the ♠A, you will still need two tricks in diamonds to beat this contract. You must hope partner has the ◊K.

Lesson 8

OPENING BIDS OF MORE THAN ONE OF A SUIT

SCORING

Opening bids of TWO OF A SUIT show hands with which opener expects to make game or slam regardless of responder's holding. The requirements for this action are:

REQUIREMENTS FOR A STRONG TWO-BID

1. Enough certain PLAYING TRICKS in hand to make game.
2. At least four QUICK TRICKS.

Note that we have not specified a certain number of high-card points.

Since opener's strong two-bid promises that game is certain, responder MUST NOT PASS. *You must respond,* even with a worthless hand. Remember that opener bid two, not just one, to prevent you from passing with weakness. After an opening two-bid, the auction must not die until game is reached or the opponents are doubled.

In responding to partner's opening two-bid, your options are:

STRONG TWO-BIDS.

79

RESPONSES TO A STRONG TWO-BID

1. 2 NT, which shows weakness, generally fewer than 7 high-card points.
2. A JUMP TO GAME IN PARTNER'S SUIT, which shows good support for his suit but no outside ace, king, singleton or void.

Any other response is *positive* and promises at least 7 points and some possible tricks. You would have responded to an opening one-bid, and a slam is possible.

3. A SINGLE RAISE OF PARTNER'S SUIT shows 7+ high-card points and support for his suit.
4. A NEW-SUIT BID show 7+ high-card points and a five-card or longer suit with some honors.

Opening bids of THREE OR MORE are preemptive, designed to crowd the bidding and prevent the opponents from exchanging information and bidding accurately. Preemptive openings are good tactics when you have the right kind of hand to use them. The best time to preempt is:

WHEN TO PREEMPT

1. When your hand offers little defense.
2. When you hold a long, strong suit (typically, seven cards when you preempt at the three level, eight or nine cards if you preempt at an even higher level) that you can rely on for tricks if your suit is trumps.
3. When the vulnerability is in your favor (you are not vulnerable, they are).

When your partner opens with a preemptive bid below game,

you can count on him for six or seven sure tricks. With four sure tricks in your own hand, therefore, raise him to game.

SCORING AT RUBBER BRIDGE

TRICK SCORE — what you score for the tricks you bid and make as well as overtricks.

In spades/hearts   30 per trick
In clubs/diamonds 20 per trick
In notrump   40 for the first trick, 30 for every trick thereafter

If the contract is played doubled and made, multiply the usual trick score by two. If it is played doubled and redoubled and made, multiply the usual trick score by four.

To score game, you need 100 or more points in trick scores "below the line."

BONUSES —

Rubber bonus   500 if you make two games out of three
                700 if you make two games and the opponents do not make a game

Slam bonuses   500 for a small slam, not vulnerable
                750 for a small slam, vulnerable*
                1000 for a grand slam, not vulnerable
                1500 for a grand slam, vulnerable

Honors   100 for four trump honors in one hand
                150 for all five trump honors in one hand
                150 for all four aces in one hand at notrump.
                (The honor bonuses may be claimed by a defender.)

---
*Vulnerable means the partnership has won a game.

For making a doubled contract	50
For making a redoubled contract	100

For doubled and	100 per trick doubled, not vulnerable
redoubled	200 per trick doubled, vulnerable
overtricks	200 per trick redoubled, not vulnerable
	400 per trick redoubled, vulnerable

PENALTIES — what you score if you set the opponents' contract:

> 50 per trick, undoubled, not vulnerable
> 100 for first trick, doubled, not vulnerable
> 200 for second trick, doubled, not vulnerable
> 200 for third trick, doubled, not vulnerable
> 300 for every trick thereafter, doubled, not vulnerable
> 100 per trick, undoubled, vulnerable
> 200 for first trick, doubled, vulnerable
> 300 for every trick thereafter, doubled, vulnerable.

If redoubled, multiply the doubled penalty by two.

QUIZ ON OPENING BIDS OF MORE THAN ONE:

I. You are the dealer, with neither side vulnerable. What is your action with each of these hands?

1. ♠ AKx
   ♡ Ax
   ◊ AKxxxxx
   ♣ x

2. ♠ AJx
   ♡ Axx
   ◊ AKxx
   ♣ KQx

3. ♠ AKQxxx
   ♡ Axx
   ◊ Kxx
   ♣ x

4. ♠ AKQxx
   ♡ AKQxx
   ◇ —
   ♣ Qxx

5. ♠ AJx
   ♡ KQx
   ◇ AKxxx
   ♣ KQ

6. ♠ —
   ♡ xxx
   ◇ xx
   ♣ KQJxxxxx

7. ♠ Axxxxxx
   ♡ Qx
   ◇ xx
   ♣ xx

8. ♠ QJ10xxxx
   ♡ x
   ◇ Kxxx
   ♣ x

9. ♠ AQJxxxx
   ♡ Qx
   ◇ KJx
   ♣ x

10. ♠ x
    ♡ xxx
    ◇ AK
    ♣ Jxxxxx

11. ♠ KJxxxxx
    ♡ Qx
    ◇ Kx
    ♣ Qx

12. ♠ KQJxxxxx
    ♡ —
    ◇ xxx
    ♣ Qx

13. ♠ AQxx
    ♡ xx
    ◇ AKQ
    ♣ Axxx

14. ♠ x
    ♡ xx
    ◇ AQJxxxx
    ♣ Qxx

15. ♠ AKQxxx
    ♡ AKxx
    ◇ —
    ♣ KQx

II. Partner opens 2♡ and your right-hand opponent passes
What is your response with each of these hands?

1. ♠ xxxx
   ♡ x
   ◇ xxxx
   ♣ xxxx

2. ♠ KJxxx
   ♡ xx
   ◇ xxx
   ♣ xxx

3. ♠ Qxxx
   ♡ Jx
   ◇ Qxx
   ♣ Jxxx

4. ♠ Ax
   ♡ KJx
   ◇ xxxx
   ♣ xxxx

5. ♠ AK
   ♡ KJx
   ◇ Jxxxx
   ♣ xxx

6. ♠ xx
   ♡ QJxxx
   ◇ xxxx
   ♣ xx

7. ♠ xx
   ♡ Jxx
   ◇ Kxxx
   ♣ xxxx

8. ♠ KQJxx
   ♡ xx
   ◇ Kxx
   ♣ xxx

9. ♠ Axx
   ♡ x
   ◇ AJxxx
   ♣ xxxx

83

10. ♠ xx
    ♡ Kx
    ♢ xxx
    ♣ Q10xxxx

III. Partner opens 3♠ and your right-hand opponent passes. What action do you take with each of these hands?

1. ♠ x
   ♡ AKxx
   ♢ Axxx
   ♣ AJxx

2. ♠ xxx
   ♡ Kxx
   ♢ Axxx
   ♣ QJx

3. ♠ Axx
   ♡ QJxx
   ♢ KJx
   ♣ AKx

4. ♠ Ax
   ♡ xx
   ♢ AKxxx
   ♣ KJxx

SOLUTIONS TO QUIZ ON OPENING BIDS OF MORE THAN ONE:

I. 1. 2♢
    2. 1♢
    3. 1♠
    4. 2♠
    5. 2 NT
    6. 4♣
    7. Pass
    8. 3♠

    9. 1♠
    10. Pass
    11. Pass
    12. 4♠
    13. 1♣
    14. 3♢
    15. 2♠

II. 1. 2 NT. You must respond.
    2. 2 NT. Too weak to bid 2♠.
    3. 2 NT
    4. 3♡
    5. 3♡. Slam is almost certain.

84

6. 4♡, showing good support and nothing else.
7. 2 NT, planning to raise hearts next.
8. 2♠
9. 3◊
10. 2 NT. Too weak to bid 3♣.

III. 1. 4♠. You have the tricks to raise. Support for partner's suit is not needed.
2. Pass
3. 3 NT. You hope to run partner's spade suit. You might be off four fast tricks in a 4♠ contract.
4. 4♠

QUIZ ON RUBBER BRIDGE SCORING:

I. You are the scorekeeper. Keep a score diagram for the following imaginary rubber.

HAND 1: WE play 4♠ and make five.
HAND 2: THEY play 2♣ and make four, with a hundred honors.
HAND 3: THEY play 3◊ doubled, down one.
HAND 4: WE play 3 NT, down two.
HAND 5: THEY play 1♠ and make three.
HAND 6: WE play 4♠ doubled and redoubled, down two.
HAND 7: WE play 3♡ doubled, making four.

II. You are the scorekeeper. Keep a scoring diagram for the following imaginary rubber.

HAND 1: WE play 3♡, making five.
HAND 2: THEY play 3 NT, making four.
HAND 3: WE play 4♠ doubled, down three, with a hundred and fifty honors.
HAND 4: THEY play 2◊, making three.

HAND 5: WE play 6♠, making six.
HAND 6: WE play 5♣ doubled, down one.
HAND 7: THEY play 7◊, making seven.

III. Answer the following questions. Try not to refer to the scoring outline.

1. How many points do diamonds score per trick bid and made?
2. How many points are needed to score a game?
3. How many points does notrump score per trick bid and made?
4. What is the rubber bonus for winning two games in a row?
5. What is the bonus for a small slam, vulnerable?
6. How many points are scored for four trump honors in one hand?
7. What do you score for making a doubled contract?
8. What is the penalty for a one-trick set, undoubled, not vulnerable?
9. What is the penalty for a three-trick set, undoubled, vulnerable?
10. What is the penalty for a four-trick set, doubled, not vulnerable?

SOLUTIONS TO QUIZ ON
RUBBER BRIDGE SCORING:

I.

WE	THEY
700	1000
50	60
200	200
100	100
30	40
120	
180	40
	30
1380	1470

THEY win the rubber by 90 points, usually rounded off to the nearest hundred. You would say, "THEY won a one."

II.

WE	THEY
	1500
	500
	200
500	20
150	500
60	30
90	100
180	40
	140
980	3030

THEY "won a twenty-one."

III. 1. 20
2. 100
3. 40 for the first trick, 30 for every subsequent trick.
4. 700
5. 750
6. 100
7. 50, plus the usual trick score is doubled, plus whatever bonuses may apply.
8. 50
9. 300
10. 800

INTRODUCTION TO DEFENSIVE PLAY: OPENING LEADS

(Before studying this section, review the introductory material on opening leads in Lesson 3.)

CHOOSING A SUIT TO LEAD; CHOOSING AN OPENING LEAD

AGAINST NOTRUMP CONTRACTS:

Usually you begin by leading your LONGEST suit, hoping to get the long cards established. With two suits of equal length, lead the stronger suit. Continue to lead the same suit at every opportunity. However . . .

If partner has bid a suit, particularly if he has opened the bidding in a major suit or overcalled in any suit, he is likely to have a good suit. Lead his suit unless you have a very strong suit of your own and an entry.

If your hand is very weak, you may speculate on what suit your partner might have length in and lead that suit, even though partner has not bid.

AGAINST SUIT CONTRACTS:

Several holdings may provide an attractive lead. Following is a list, with the most desirable leads at the top of the list.

LEADS AGAINST SUIT CONTRACTS

1. A suit your partner has bid, particularly if he overcalled.*
2. A strong sequence, like KQJx or QJ10x.
3. A singleton (not in trumps).
4. A suit in which you have a worthless holding. Maybe partner has some useful honors.
5. A long suit in which declarer may not have many tricks. There is no particular advantage to establishing long cards against a suit contract, since declarer will be able to trump them if they are led; but the lead of a long suit may be *safe*.

If none of these leads is available, you might:

6. Lead trumps, another lead that is safe and probably won't give declarer any tricks that aren't always his anyway.
7. Lay down an unsupported ace.
8. Gamble with a lead like the queen from Qx, hoping to find something really good in partner's hand.
9. Lead a suit the opponents have not bid, regardless of your holding.
10. Lead through the strength of dummy's first-bid suit.

ALWAYS TAKE THE STRENGTHS AND WEAKNESSES OF DUMMY INTO ACCOUNT WHEN YOU ARE SELECTING A SUIT TO LEAD. REMEMBER OUR STRATEGY OF LEADING THROUGH STRENGTH AND UP TO WEAKNESS.

---

*We'll cover overcalls in detail next lesson.

OPENING LEADS:

If your right-hand opponent is declarer, you must make the opening lead *before* you see dummy. This is why opening leads are a difficult part of defensive play.

Any of the suggested leads might make a reasonable opening lead, particularly the lead from a good *sequence*. The lead of a suit headed by the ace-king is perhaps the best sequential lead of all. You can expect to win the first trick, and you may be able to better judge what to lead next *after* you see the dummy.

Of course, if your partner has bid, you will consider leading his suit. If he has overcalled, suggesting a good suit, you will almost always lead his suit. If he has opened the bidding, lead his suit unless you have a very attractive lead of your own (such as an ace-king, a singleton or a strong sequence).

If partner responds to your opening bid with a suit of his own, remember that he promises no special suit quality. The lead of his suit in this case is not guaranteed to be productive.

QUIZ ON OPENING LEADS:

I. The opponents have bid 1 NT - 3 NT, and you must make the opening lead. What card would you choose from each of these hands?

1. ♠ K J 8 6 3   2. ♠ K J 6 2   3. ♠ 7 5
   ♡ A 5 4   ♡ A 8   ♡ A 9 7 5 2
   ◇ 6 4   ◇ K 10 8 6 3   ◇ 8 7 4
   ♣ 10 5 3   ♣ 6 5   ♣ A K 4

4. ♠ 7 6 3   5. ♠ Q J 10 5
   ♡ J 10   ♡ 8 4
   ◇ J 9 7 6 2   ◇ 8 7 3
   ♣ 8 7 4   ♣ K 9 8 3

II. The auction has gone:

LHO	Partner	RHO	You
1♣	1♡	1♠	Pass
2♣	Pass	3 NT	Pass
Pass	Pass		

You must make the opening lead. What card would you choose from each of these hands?

1. ♠ 8 6 3
   ♡ J 6
   ◊ 8 7 6
   ♣ J 9 6 4 2

2. ♠ K J 9 7 3
   ♡ Q 7
   ◊ 8 5
   ♣ 9 7 6 3

3. ♠ 8 7 3 2
   ♡ 8
   ◊ A J 9 6 4
   ♣ 8 7 6

4. ♠ A 8 6 2
   ♡ Q 9 2
   ◊ 8 6
   ♣ 9 7 6 2

5. ♠ 8 6 5 3
   ♡ 10 3
   ◊ A 9 7 5 4 2
   ♣ 8

III. The opponents have bid 1♡ - 3♡ - 4♡. You must make the opening lead. What card would you choose from each of these hands?

1. ♠ A K 7
   ♡ 7 6
   ◊ Q 9 7 3
   ♣ 10 8 6 3

2. ♠ K Q 10 4
   ♡ 8 7 5
   ◊ J 9 5 3
   ♣ A 7

3. ♠ 9 8 6 4
   ♡ A 8 6
   ◊ 5
   ♣ Q 8 7 6 2

4. ♠ K 7 6
   ♡ 6 5
   ◊ K 7 6
   ♣ 9 7 6 5 2

5. ♠ Q 10 4 2
   ♡ 8 7 5
   ◊ K 9 6
   ♣ A 8 6

IV. Partner opened 1 ♠, right-hand opponent overcalled 2 ♡, left-hand opponent raised to 4 ♡, passed out. What opening lead would you choose from each of these hands?

1. ♠ Q 5
   ♡ 7 6 3
   ◇ J 10 9 4
   ♣ 6 5 4 3

2. ♠ Q 8 6 4
   ♡ 8 7 4
   ◇ 4
   ♣ 10 8 6 5 2

3. ♠ J 8
   ♡ 7 6 5
   ◇ A K 4
   ♣ 9 7 6 5 2

4. ♠ 10 6 4
   ♡ 8 7
   ◇ K 10 8 6
   ♣ Q 10 8 7

5. ♠ 6 4 2
   ♡ 7 5 2
   ◇ Q J 10 8
   ♣ K 9 7

V. The auction has gone:

LHO	Partner	RHO	You
1♣	1♠	2♣	Pass
2 NT	Pass	3♡	Pass
4♡	Pass	Pass	Pass

You must make the opening lead against this contract. What card would you choose from each of these hands?

1. ♠ J 8
   ♡ 7 6 5
   ◇ Q J 10 9 4
   ♣ 8 7 4

2. ♠ A 7
   ♡ 8 7 6
   ◇ 10 9 8 6 4
   ♣ K 7 4

3. ♠ Q 9 2
   ♡ 9 8 6
   ◇ A 8 7 5
   ♣ 7 6 5

4. ♠ Q 5
   ♡ 9 8 6 3
   ◇ A K 5
   ♣ 9 7 6 3

5. ♠ J 8 6
   ♡ 7 6
   ◇ 8 7 5 3
   ♣ A 8 6 5

VI. The auction has gone:

LHO	Partner	RHO	You
1 ◇	Pass	1 ♠	Pass
2 ♠	Pass	4 ♠	Pass
Pass	Pass		

You must make the opening lead. What card would you choose from each of these hands?

1. ♠ 6 4
   ♡ K Q J 8
   ◇ A 7 4
   ♣ J 9 7 5

2. ♠ Q 7 5
   ♡ K 7 6 3
   ◇ 9 8 7
   ♣ K 8 6

3. ♠ A 7 5
   ♡ 5
   ◇ J 8 6 4
   ♣ J 8 7 6 3

4. ♠ A 8 6
   ♡ 8 6
   ◇ A 8 7 5
   ♣ J 10 9 4

5. ♠ A 6
   ♡ J 9 7 6 4
   ◇ K 10 4 2
   ♣ Q 7

SOLUTIONS TO QUIZ ON OPENING LEADS:

I. 1. ♠ 6.
    2. ◇ 6; lead your longest suit, even though your spades are stronger.
    3. ♡ 5; do not cash your high clubs; you may need them as entries to lead your long suit again.
    4. ♡ J; your hand is so weak, without a single entry, that you should try to find partner's long suit.
    5. ♠ Q.

II. 1. ♡ J.
    2. ♡ Q. Do not lead your own suit when partner has suggested a good suit with his overcall. Also, your right-hand opponent showed length in spades

3. ♦ 6, with only a singleton in partner's suit. Note you need only a little help to establish your suit.

4. ♡ 2.

5. ♡ 10. The quality of your diamond suit is too poor to consider leading it.

III. 1. ♠ A.

2. ♠ K.

3. ♦ 5. Perhaps partner has the ace and will win and return the suit for you to trump.

4. ♣ 5. The lead of a worthless suit can be effective, since you might be leading to some honors in partner's hand. You might help declarer if you lead from either of your kings.

5. ♡ 5. Lead a trump, for safety, since you have no attractive lead in any other suit.

IV. 1. ♠ Q.

2. ♦ 4; partner has a good hand for his opening; perhaps he has the ♦ A (or ♡ A!)

3. ♦ A.

4. ♡ 7. Sometimes a trump is a good lead because it is relatively safe, unlikely to give away a trick. Often a trump lead by the defense will hurt declarer's cause by preventing him from making extra tricks by using his trumps separately. You draw two of declarer's trumps with your lead. Here, partner has the spades and you have tricks in the minor suits. So declarer will try for his contract by making extra trump tricks.

5. ♦ Q.

V. 1. ♠ J; almost always lead partner's suit when he overcalls.

2. ♠ A.

3. ♠ 2.

4. ◇A, although the ♠Q is a close second choice.
5. ♣A. This is a rare exception. You plan to lead another club after taking your ace, expecting partner to trump! The opponents bid and raised clubs before they settled into hearts, so partner should have one club at most.

VI. 1. ♡K.
2. ◇9. No other lead is particularly attractive. A diamond lead looks safe.
3. ♡5; hoping to trump further heart leads.
4. ♣J.
5. ♡6. The lead of your longest suit here looks safest. Declarer probably is short in this suit, so your lead will be of no help to him.

Lesson 9

WHEN THE OPPONENTS OPEN THE BIDDING

There are many good reasons why you may wish to bid even though your opponents have made the first bid in the auction. You may still find a makable contract; make it more difficult for the opponents to bid accurately or drive them up to a level where they may be set; or indicate a good suit for your partner to lead if your side winds up defending.

However, it is also dangerous to enter the auction when your opponents have opened, mainly because they may double you and set you badly. To lessen this risk, almost any action you take after the opponents have opened is based on the possession of a good suit or good prospects of finding a playable suit. If you have good trumps, you are assured of some tricks and your chances of suffering a heavy penalty are lessened.

Here are your options if your right-hand opponent opens the bidding:

YOU CAN STILL HAVE A HAPPY RESULT EVEN THOUGH THE OPPONENTS BID FIRST.

ACTIONS AFTER THE OPPONENTS
OPEN THE BIDDING

PASS

This may be right even if you have an opening bid (or even more) in high cards. If you do not have a good suit and no prospects of locating one, it may be too dangerous for you to enter the auction. You are not obliged to bid with 13 points after the opponents have opened.

OVERCALL

With a good suit, always five or more cards long, and about an opening bid or slightly more.

JUMP OVERCALL

With a good six-card suit but a poor hand. This bid is used as a mild preempt.

PREEMPT

With a good seven-card suit or longer just as you would do as opener. Pay attention, however, to the vulnerability.

MAKE A TAKEOUT DOUBLE

With either (1) an opening bid or better plus support for all the unbid suits, or (2) a powerful hand, 18 points or more, plus a good suit of your own.

OVERCALL 1 NT

With 16-18 high-card points and some high cards in the opponents' suit.

CUEBID THE OPPONENTS' SUIT

With a hand that you would have opened with a forcing two-bid.

A TAKEOUT DOUBLE helps you find your best trump suit when you have at least three cards in each of the unbid suits and you want your partner to choose a suit. The options available in RESPONDING TO A TAKEOUT DOUBLE:

RESPONSES TO A TAKEOUT DOUBLE

With 0-9 points	—bid a suit as cheaply as possible. —bid 1 NT with a balanced hand and some high cards in the opponents' suit.
With 10-12 points	—jump in your best suit to invite game. —jump to 2 NT with balanced pattern and some high cards in the opponents' suit to invite game in notrump.
With 13 points or more	—jump to game in your best suit. —jump to 3 NT with balanced pattern and some high cards in the opponents' suit.

There is actually a third option if you have a very strong hand — a CUEBID OF THE OPPONENTS' SUIT can be used to show a desire to bid game but doubt as to which game contract is best.

DO NOT PASS a takeout double without a fair hand and a LONG, SOLID HOLDING IN THE OPPONENTS' SUIT.

AFTER YOU HAVE MADE A TAKEOUT DOUBLE, DO NOT BID AGAIN UNLESS YOU HAVE AT LEAST 17 POINTS. PARTNER HAS BEEN FORCED TO RESPOND AND MAY HAVE A VERY POOR HAND.

QUIZ ON ACTING OVER THE OPPONENTS' OPENING BID:

I. With neither side vulnerable your right-hand opponent opened the bidding with 1 ◇. What should you do with these hands?

1. ♠ Axx
   ♡ Kxx
   ◇ Qxx
   ♣ AJxx

2. ♠ xx
   ♡ Axx
   ◇ KQ10x
   ♣ Axxx

3. ♠ AQJxx
   ♡ Axx
   ◇ xx
   ♣ Jxx

4. ♠ xx
   ♡ Ax
   ◇ Qxxx
   ♣ KJxxx

5. ♠ KQ10xxx
   ♡ x
   ◇ xx
   ♣ J10xx

6. ♠ x
   ♡ KQJxxxx
   ◇ xx
   ♣ Jxx

7. ♠ Kxxx
   ♡ Axx
   ◇ xx
   ♣ AQxx

8. ♠ AK
   ♡ AQJxx
   ◇ xx
   ♣ Axxx

9. ♠ Ax
   ♡ Kxx
   ◇ AJx
   ♣ KQxxx

10. ♠ AKJxx
    ♡ AKQxx
    ◇ x
    ♣ Kx

QUIZ ON RESPONDING TO A TAKEOUT DOUBLE:

II. Your left-hand opponent opened 1♣, and your partner doubled for takeout. What should you do with these hands:

1. ♠ Qxxx
   ♡ xxx
   ◇ xx
   ♣ xxxx

2. ♠ Qxxx
   ♡ Qx
   ◇ xx
   ♣ Jxxxx

3. ♠ AQxx
   ♡ xx
   ◇ AJx
   ♣ xxxx

4. ♠ Axxxx   5. ♠ xx   6. ♠ xx
    ♡ AK   ♡ Kxx   ♡ Axx
    ◊ Jxx   ◊ Qxxx   ◊ Kxxx
    ♣ xxx   ♣ Kxxx   ♣ KJxx

7. ♠ Jx   8. ♠ xx   9. ♠ xx
    ♡ Jxx   ♡ Axx   ♡ Axx
    ◊ KJxxxx   ◊ Kxx   ◊ KQJxx
    ♣ AQ   ♣ KJ1098   ♣ xxx

10. ♠ Kxx
     ♡ AKx
     ◊ Axxxx
     ♣ xx

QUIZ ON REBIDDING AFTER YOU MADE A TAKEOUT DOUBLE:

III. Your right-hand opponent has opened 1 ♡, you doubled for takeout, and your partner responded 1 ♠. What should you do with:

1. ♠ AKJx   2. ♠ AQxx   3. ♠ AQxx
    ♡ xx   ♡ x   ♡ x
    ◊ Kxxx   ◊ AKxx   ◊ AKQx
    ♣ Qxx   ♣ Kxxx   ♣ KQJx

4. ♠ AJx
    ♡ xx
    ◊ AKx
    ♣ KQJxx

SOLUTIONS TO QUIZZES:

I.		II.		III.	
1.	Pass	1.	1♠	1.	Pass
2.	Pass	2.	1♠	2.	2♠
3.	1♠	3.	2♠	3.	4♠
4.	Pass	4.	4♠	4.	2♣
5.	2♠	5.	1 NT		
6.	3♡	6.	2 NT		
7.	Double	7.	3 NT		
8.	Double	8.	Pass		
9.	1 NT	9.	2♢		
10.	2♢	10.	2♣. Game is certain, but you are uncertain as to the proper strain.		

WE'RE GLAD YOU GOT ALL
THE QUIZ QUESTIONS CORRECT!

Lesson 10

THE CHALLENGE OF BRIDGE

We have been learning a great many *rules* that govern proper bidding, play and defense. There is, however, a lot more to playing and enjoying bridge than strict adherence to a set of rules. When you sit down to play bridge, you have a chance to display creativity, imagination and logical thought. This is a thinking person's game.

Following are some hands, presented in quiz form, that illustrate some of the fine points of bridge. Look at these problems and try to solve some of them. Don't be discouraged if you find them too difficult. Even an experienced player would probably fail to get them all right. The problems are not intended to show you how much you still have to learn, but to offer you inspiration for the future.

Bridge can be an exhilarating and rewarding game to play well. We hope these hands will demonstrate that there are some worthy goals for you to pursue in becoming a bridge player.

QUIZ ON THE CHALLENGE OF BRIDGE:

1.
> ♠ x x x
> ♡ J 9 x
> ◇ K Q J x
> ♣ A x x
>
> ♠ A Q 10
> ♡ A 10 x
> ◇ A x x x
> ♣ Q x x

Contract: 3 NT
West leads a low spade, East plays the jack, and you win the queen. How do you play to make your contract for certain?

102

2.

    ♠ x x x
    ♡ Q x
    ◇ A Q 6 5 3
    ♣ J x x

    ♠ A K x
    ♡ A x x
    ◇ K 9 7 4
    ♣ A x x

Contract: 3 NT

West leads the ♡J. You try dummy's queen, but East covers with the king, and you win the ace. How do you play from here?

3.

    ♠ x x
    ♡ x x x
    ◇ Q J x x
    ♣ A K x x

    ♠ A K J
    ♡ Q x
    ◇ A 10 x x x
    ♣ Q x x

Contract: 3 NT

West leads a low spade and East plays the ten. What is your best chance to make this contract?

4. ♠ A x x
    ♡ A J x x
    ◊ x x x
    ♣ A K 10

    ♠ K Q 10 x x x
    ♡ Q x
    ◊ x x x
    ♣ x x

You reach a 4♠ contract after East opens the bidding with 1 NT
(16-18 HCP). West leads the ◊J. East cashes the ace, king,
and queen, and shifts to a trump. How should you play?

5. ♠ K x
    ♡ x x x x x
    ◊ x x x x
    ♣ x x

    ♠ A Q x x x
    ♡ A K Q
    ◊ A Q x
    ♣ A x

Contract: 3 NT
West leads a low club. East plays the queen and you win. You
try hearts, but West discards on the second round. What should
you do now?

6.
        ♠ x x x
        ♡ K 9
        ◊ x x x x
        ♣ Q x x x

        ♠ A Q J
        ♡ A Q J x x x x
        ◊ x x
        ♣ x

Contract: 4 ♡
West leads the ♣ J and you trump the second round of clubs.
What is your best chance to make this contract?

7.
        ♠ A x x x
        ♡ J 10 x x
        ◊ K x x
        ♣ x x

        ♠ J x
        ♡ A Q 9 x x
        ◊ A Q x
        ♣ K J x

Contract: 4 ♡
You opened 1 ♡ *after three passes* and got to game in hearts.
West leads the ♠ K. You win the ace and take a heart finesse,
losing to West's king. West cashes the ♠ Q, and you ruff the
next spade and draw trumps. Now should you lead a club to
your king or a club to your jack?

8

♠ K x
♡ J x x
◇ J x x
♣ K J x x x

♠ x x
♡ K Q 10 x x x
◇ A
♣ A 10 x x

Contract: 4 ♡

East opened the bidding 1 ♠. West leads a spade, and East wins the queen and ace. East cashes the ace of trumps and gets out with a trump, West following. With the trumps in, you play a club to the king, both opponents playing low, and a club back, East playing the nine. Do you play your ace or finesse your ten?

SOLUTIONS TO QUIZ ON
THE CHALLENGE OF BRIDGE:

1. Cash enough diamond tricks to exhaust the opponents of that suit. Then lead a heart from dummy and play the ten from your hand (unless East plays an honor). If West wins the heart trick, he will be ENDPLAYED, forced to give you an extra trick no matter what suit he returns. Try out the various possibilities and see for yourself.

2. You must be careful to lead one of your *middle diamond spots* when you begin to cash your diamond tricks, to UNBLOCK this blocked suit. If the missing diamonds are divided 3-1 you must *save* your ◇4 to play underneath dummy's five or six, allowing you to cash the fifth diamond.

3. Win the first trick with the *king*. Then lead a club to dummy and try the diamond finesse. If it loses, you hope that West will lead spades again instead of shifting to a

heart. If you win the first spade with the jack, West will know there is no future for his side of spades.

4. Cash the ♡A and *run off all your trumps*. East, who must hold all the missing high cards for his 1 NT opening, will be SQUEEZED in hearts and clubs. He won't be able to hold his ♡K and his club stopper. Try it and see for yourself.

5. Play a spade to the king and try the diamond finesse. This gives you a 50% chance of making your bid. The alternative is to try to find the spades split 3-3, but that will happen only about one-third of the time.

6. You need to take *two* spade finesses and require *two* entries to dummy. Lead a heart to dummy's nine, taking a strange finesse in a suit in which you have almost all the high cards, hoping to get the extra entry you need.

7. Lead a club to your *king*. West would probably have opened the bidding with the ♠KQ, the ♡K, *and* the ♣A. So the ♣A should be on your right.

8. Play the ♣A. If you finesse the ♣10, you are playing East for ♣Q9x and West for a singleton. But West would probably had *led* a singleton club against this contract if he had one. That would be a very attractive line of defense to anyone. So the clubs are very likely divided 2-2, and the queen will fall under your ace.

COMPREHENSIVE GLOSSARY

"ABOVE THE LINE": Scoring of points won for overtricks, penalties and bonuses.

ACTIVE DEFENSE: The defenders' approach when they are desperate for tricks because declarer threatens to get discards for his losers.

ASSUMPTION: Technique by which declarer or a defender bases his play on the premise that the contract can be made or set.

ATTITUDE: Defensive signal that shows like or dislike for a suit.

AVOIDANCE: Technique in play whereby a dangerous opponent is kept from gaining the lead.

AUCTION: See BIDDING.

BALANCED HAND: Hand containing no void suit or singleton, and no more than one doubleton.

BALANCING: Backing into the auction after the opponents have stopped low, counting on partner to hold some values.

"BELOW THE LINE": Scoring of points that count toward making a game.

BID: Call in the auction that promises to take a certain number of tricks in the play and suggests a suit as trumps (or suggests the play be at notrump).

BIDDING: The first phase of each hand of bridge, when the players on both sides have a chance to name the trump suit and suggest how many tricks they expect their side to win in the play.

BLACKWOOD:	A conventional bid of 4 NT that asks partner to reveal, through an artificial response, the number of aces he holds.
BOOK:	(1) The first six tricks won by declarer's side; (2) the number of tricks the defenders must win before they begin to score undertricks.
BROKEN SEQUENCE:	Sequence such as QJ9, which contains a gap between the middle and lowest of the three cards.
BROKEN SUIT:	Suit that contains no cards adjacent in rank.
BUSINESS DOUBLE:	Penalty double.
CALL:	Any action, including a pass, taken in the bidding.
CAPTAINCY:	The bidding principle whereby one partner is obliged to take responsibility for placing the contract once his partner's hand is limited in strength.
CARD SENSE:	An intangible quality that those skilled in card play seem to possess.
CHICAGO SCORING:	A type of scoring in which every deal is taken as a separate entity. There are no rubbers or partscores carried over to the next deal.
COME-ON:	An encouraging attitude signal.
COMPETITIVE BIDDING:	Auctions in which both sides bid.

CONSTRUCTIVE BIDDING:	Auctions in which one side tries to reach its best contract without interference.
CONTRACT:	The number of tricks the side that wins the auction undertakes to make.
CONTROL:	Holding that prevents the opponents from taking two fast tricks in that suit. An ace; king; or singleton or void, if some other suit is trumps.
CONVENTION:	A bid to which an artificial meaning is assigned.
CROSS-RUFF:	A play technique in which cards are trumped in both partnership hands alternately on several successive tricks.
CUEBID:	(1) A bid of an opponent's suit, intended to show great strength.
	(2) A bid of a suit in which a control is held, intended to facilitate slam investigation.
	(3) Any of several conventional cuebids, such as Michaels.
CUT:	The division of the pack into rough halves prior to the deal.
DEAL:	The distribution of the 52 cards, 13 to each player face down, that begins each hand of bridge.
DECLARER:	The player who tries to make the contract by using both his own and dummy's cards.
DEFENDERS:	The partnership that opposes declarer and tries to defeat the contract.

DISCARD:	A played card that is not of the suit led nor of the trump suit.
DOUBLE FINESSE:	A combination of plays in which declarer finesses against two missing honors.
DOUBLE SQUEEZE:	An advanced type of squeeze in which each defender is squeezed in turn.
DOUBLETON:	A holding of two cards in a suit.
DOUBLE:	A call generally intended to increase the penalty suffered by the opponents if their last bid becomes an unsuccessful contract.
DRAW TRUMPS:	Technique in which declarer leads trumps, forcing the opponents to follow suit, until their trumps are exhausted.
DROP:	Cause a missing high card to fall by playing a still higher card or cards.
DUMMY:	Declarer's partner. The term is also applied to the dummy's cards, placed face up on the table.
DUMMY REVERSAL:	Technique by which declarer makes extra tricks by ruffing several times in his own hand and ultimately drawing trumps with dummy's trump holding.
DUPLICATE BRIDGE:	A contest in which the same hands are played several times by different players, allowing for a comparison of results.
DUPLICATION OF VALUES:	The condition in which the high cards and distribution of the partnership hands are ill-suited to each other.
ECHO:	A high-low sequence of play used by a defender to signal attitude or count.

111

ENDPLAY:	Technique by which a trick is gained through deliberately giving an opponent the lead in a position where he has no safe exit.
ENTRY:	A card used as a means of gaining the lead.
EQUALS:	Cards that are adjacent in rank, or that become adjacent when the cards that separate them are played.
FALSE CARD:	A card played with intent to deceive.
FALSE PREFERENCE:	A preference offered without true support, typically with two cards.
FINESSE:	Maneuver by which it is hoped to win a trick with an intermediate card, by playing that card after one opponent has already played.
FIT:	A holding that suggests the suit will adequately serve as trumps.
FIVE-CARD MAJORS:	A bidding style in which an opening bid of 1♠ or 1♡ promises five or more cards.
FOLLOWING SUIT:	Each player's first obligation in the play, to play a card of the same suit that was led to the trick if possible.
FORCING BID:	A bid that compels partner to take further action.
FORCING DEFENSE:	The defenders' approach when they try to exhaust declarer of his trumps by repeatedly forcing him to ruff.

FORCING PASS: Pass made over an opponent's bid, which compels partner to double the opponents or bid further.

FREE BID: Bid made when the alternative would be to pass and allow partner the next opportunity to act. Typically based on sound values.

FREE RAISE: Raise of partner's suit in competition. Not a significant term, since such a raise does *not* imply extra strength.

GAME: (1) A unit of scoring, two of which comprise a rubber; a game is won by the first partnership to score 100 or more points below the line.
(2) Any contract that will allow the partnership to score game if fulfilled.

GAME TRY: A bid that suggests interest in game and asks partner to assess his values and make the final decision.

GERBER: A conventional bid of 4 ♣ that asks partner to reveal, through an artificial response, the number of aces he holds.

GRAND SLAM FORCE: A bid of 5 NT, when used to show interest in bidding a grand slam in the agreed trump suit provided partner holds certain honors in trumps.

HIGH-CARD POINT COUNT: Method of hand evaluation in which a numerical value is assigned to each high honor.

HONOR: Ace, king, queen, jack or ten.

HONORS:	Bonus available in the scoring for a holding of four or all five honors in the trump suit in the same hand; or, at notrump, all four aces in the same hand.
HOLD-UP:	Refusal to take a winner, often for purposes of disrupting the opponents' communication.
INFERENCE:	A conclusion logically deduced from evidence.
INFERENTIAL COUNT:	An assessment of the entire distribution of the concealed hands, based on evidence from the bidding and the early play.
INTERIOR SEQUENCE:	Holding such as KJ109x, in which the equals are accompanied by a higher honor.
INTERMEDIATES:	Cards that may become winners as the cards that outrank them are played.
INVITATIONAL BID:	Bid that asks partner to continue to game or slam with maximum values.
JORDAN:	The conventional understanding in which a jump to 2 NT by responder, after the opening bid is doubled for takeout, shows a limit raise in opener's suit.
JUMP OVERCALL:	A suit bid usually made (as the next bid) after an opponent has opened the bidding, but at a higher level than necessary.
JUMP SHIFT:	(1) A jump of one level in a new suit by opening bidder. (2) A jump of one level in a new suit by responder. Either action implies great strength.

LEG:	A fulfilled partscore, a step toward game.
LEAD:	The first card played to a trick.
LIMIT BID:	Bid that promises no more than a pre-agreed amount of high-card strength.
LIMIT RAISE:	Direct double raise of partner's opening one-bid that promises invitational values only.
LONG CARDS:	Low cards that become winners because they are the only cards of their suit that remain in play.
MAJOR SUITS:	Spades and hearts
MATCHPOINT SCORING:	Type of scoring used in duplicate (tournament) bridge, in which several different results from an identical deal are compared.
MAXIMUM:	Holding the greatest possible values for one's previous bidding.
MINIMUM:	Holding the fewest possible values for one's previous bidding.
NEGATIVE RESPONSE:	Bid, often artificial, that denies good values; made in response to partner's forcing action.
NOTRUMP:	Strain in which the play is conducted with no trump suit. The highest card played of the suit that is led to a trick wins that trick.
OBLIGATORY FALSECARD:	Falsecard that will lead to a certain loss if not played.

OBLIGATORY FINESSE:	The handling of certain suit combinations in which declarer plays a low card from both hands, hoping his opponent will be forced to follow suit with a high honor.
OFFSIDE:	Unfavorably placed for a finesse to work.
ONSIDE:	Favorably placed for a finesse to work.
OPEN THE BIDDING:	To make the first bid in the auction.
OPENING LEAD:	The lead to the first trick, made by the defender to declarer's left.
OVERCALL:	Bid in a suit after the opponents have opened the bidding (but before partner has taken any action).
OVERTRICKS:	Tricks taken in excess of those bid.
PARTIAL:	A partscore.
PARTNERSHIP:	Two players working as a unit. Bridge is played by two competing partnerships. Partners sit opposite each other. Trust and cooperation between partners are important features of the game.
PARTSCORE:	A contract below the level of game. Successful partscores can accumulate toward scoring game.
PASS:	Call in the auction when the player does not wish to bid, double or redouble.
PASSED OUT:	Deal on which none of the four players bid. Calls for another deal.
PASSIVE DEFENSE:	Defenders' approach when dummy is short of winners and the defense can wait on its tricks.

116

PENALTY DOUBLE:	Double made for a larger penalty, in the expectation that the contract will fail.
PERCENTAGE PLAY:	Line of play that will succeed most often, determined on only a mathematical basis.
PLAIN SUIT:	Any suit other than trumps.
POINT COUNT:	The method of hand evaluation whereby a numerical value is assigned to the possible trick-taking features of a hand.
POSITIVE RESPONSE:	Response to partner's forcing opening that promises certain good values.
PREEMPTIVE BID:	Bid made not for constructive purposes but merely to crowd the opponents and make it hard for them to bid accurately.
PREFERENCE:	A bid that chooses between two possible strains partner has offered.
PREPARED BID:	An opening bid in a low-ranking suit (often, a suit of only three cards), made so that a higher-ranking suit will provide an easy, space-saving rebid.
PRIMARY VALUES:	Aces and kings.
PROPRIETIES:	That section of the Laws of Contract Bridge that deals with ethics and etiquette.
PSYCHIC BID:	A bluff bid, made on a non-existent suit or without values, intended to intimidate the opposition.

QUANTITATIVE SLAM (GAME) TRY:	Bid that asks partner to pass or bid on, based strictly on the number of high-card values he holds .
RAISE:	A bid in the same suit (or notrump) that partner has just bid, often confirming that suit as trumps.
REBID:	(1) Bid the same suit a second time. (2) Any bid chosen at one's second turn.
REDOUBLE:	Call available in the auction that doubles, in turn, points scored if the contract is played doubled.
RESPONDER:	Opening bidder's partner.
RESTRICTED CHOICE:	A mathematical concept, based on the opponents' possible play from a holding of several equal cards, that may be helpful in determining the play of certain suit combinations.
REVERSE:	(1) A rebid in a new suit, such that the level of the contract will be increased if partner shows a preference for the first suit. (2) To bid in such a way, thereby showing a strong hand.
REVOKE:	Failure to follow suit when holding a card of the suit led.
RUBBER:	Unit of scoring in bridge, won by the side to first make two games, and carrying a large bonus.
RUFF:	To trump.

RUFF-AND-DISCARD (RUFF-SLUFF):	The lead of a suit in which both declarer and dummy are void, allowing declarer to discard a loser from the hand of his choice while he ruffs in the other.
RULE OF 11:	Device, applicable if the lead is known to be fourth highest, that may be used to make judgments in the play. Subtract the rank of the spot led from 11. The remainder shows the number of higher cards held by the hands, other than leader's.
SACRIFICE:	A deliberate overbid, but one in which declarer expects to be penalized fewer points than the opponents would score if allowed to play their own contract.
SAFETY PLAY:	The handling of a combination of cards so as to insure against a devastating loss of tricks.
SECOND HAND:	(1) The next player to have a chance to bid after the dealer. (2) The player who plays immediately after a trick is led to.
SECONDARY VALUES:	Queens and jacks.
SEMI-BALANCED HAND:	Hand which is neither balanced nor unbalanced by definition. 2-2-4-5 or 2-2-3-6 pattern.
SEQUENCE:	Three or more cards adjacent in rank, the highest one of which is an honor.
SET:	To defeat the contract.
SHORT CLUB:	See PREPARED BID.

SHUTOUT BID:	A preemptive bid.
SIGNAL:	Any of several conventional understandings through which the defenders can give each other information by means of the card they play.
SIGNOFF:	Bid suggesting that partner pass.
SIMPLE SQUEEZE:	Type of squeeze in which a single opponent is squeezed.
SINGLETON:	A holding of only one card in a suit.
SLAM:	A contract for 12 or 13 tricks, carrying a bonus in the scoring.
SPOT CARD:	Card below the rank of an honor.
SQUEEZE:	Technique, most often used by declarer, in which a defender is forced to relinquish a winner no matter what card he chooses.
STANDARD AMERICAN:	The bidding system most commonly used in America; essentially, the Goren style, with gadgets and refinements added.
STOPPER:	A card or combination of cards that threatens to produce a trick in a suit.
STRIP:	Play a suit or suits so as to make it impossible for an opponent to lead that suit or lead it safely.
SUIT-PREFERENCE SIGNAL:	Defensive signal that bears no relation to its own suit but shows interest in another, specific suit.

SURROUNDING PLAY:	Maneuver in which a defender breaks a suit by leading a high card that is part of a near-sequential holding.
SYSTEM:	The total framework in which the partnership assigns well-defined meanings to its bids and bidding sequences.
TABLE PRESENCE:	The ability to draw inferences from the extraneous things that happen at the table.
TAKEOUT DOUBLE:	Double that requests partner not to pass but to choose a suit (or notrump) to play in.
TEMPORIZE:	Bid a suit (often, an unplayable suit), in the expectation of supporting partner's suit later. May be required if no immediate raise is appropriate.
TENACE:	An honor or combination of honors that will be most valuable if the holder is fourth hand to play; e.g., AQ, KJ.
THIRD HAND:	In the auction, dealer's partner. In the play, leader's partner.
THIRD-SEAT OPENING:	An opening bid after two passes that may be based on sub-minimum values. Often it is intended as mainly lead-directing and mildly preemptive.
THROW-IN:	See ENDPLAY.
TRAP PASS:	Pass made with substantial values, including strength in the opponent's suit, in the hope of making a successful penalty double later.

TREATMENT:	A particular way of assigning a natural meaning to a bid or sequence of bids.
TRICK:	Four cards played in sequence, one by each player at the table, going clockwise.
TRUMPS:	The suit determined in the bidding to be that of the contract.
TRUMP CONTROL:	Technique by which declarer makes possession of the trump suit work to his advantage, exhausting the opponents of their trumps so he can safely establish and cash other winners.
TRUMP COUP:	The advanced play by which declarer can avoid losing a trick to an outstanding trump honor by forcing a defender to ruff and be overruffed.
TRUMP ECHO:	The high-low sequence of play in the trump suit, used in defense to show an odd number of trumps.
TRUMP PROMOTION:	Defensive technique in which declarer is forced to either ruff low and be overruffed or ruff high at the later cost of a trump trick.
TRUMP SUPPORT:	Usually four or more cards in partner's suit. Under some circumstances, three or fewer cards.
UNBALANCED HAND:	Hand containing a void suit or singleton.
UNBLOCK:	Play by declarer or defenders so as to allow the uninterrupted run of a long suit by proper management of the smaller cards.

UNDERTRICKS: Tricks that declarer has bid but fails to take.

UPPERCUT: Defensive technique in which a defender ruffs in with a trump intermediate and declarer is obliged to weaken his trump holding by overruffing.

VOID: A suit in which no cards are held.

VULNERABILITY: Condition in the scoring, achieved when one game is won toward completion of the rubber.

WEAK TWO-BID: Modern treatment in which an opening bid of 2 ♣, 2 ♡ or 2 ◊ shows a good six-card suit and about an average hand in high cards.

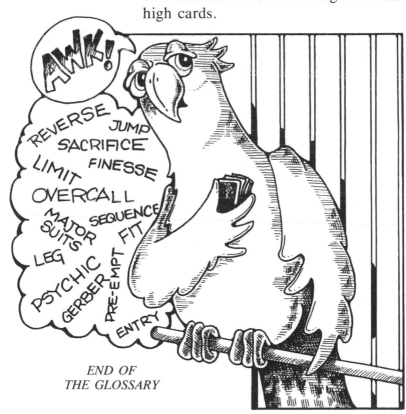

*END OF
THE GLOSSARY*

WHAT THE PROPRIETIES ARE ABOUT:

In a game such as poker, all sorts of gamesmanship is allowed. In bridge, *skill in choosing a bid or play is emphasized.* A strict code of ethics and courtesy is part of the game. The better the players in the game, the higher the standard of ethics is likely to be. A higher standard of ethics is demanded in tournament play than in a social game at home. The purpose of the *Proprieties,* that section of the Laws of bridge that deals with conduct and ethics, is to make the game more enjoyable for everyone, no matter what the situation.

Please take time to read these excerpts from the Proprieties, excerpted from the *Laws of Duplicate Contract Bridge* (1975 edition). If you observe the principles set down here, you will find yourself respected as both a partner and an opponent.

CONDUCT AND ETIQUETTE

A player should maintain at all times a courteous attitude toward his partner and the opponents. He should carefully avoid any remark or action that might cause annoyance or embarrassment to another player, or that might interfere with another player's enjoyment of the game.

As a matter of courtesy, a player should refrain from:

Paying insufficient attention;
Making gratuitous comments during the play as to the auction or the adequacy of the contract;
Detaching a card from his hand before it is his turn to play;
Arranging the cards he has played to previous tricks in a disorderly manner or mixing his cards together before the result of the deal has been agreed to;
Making a questionable claim or concession; or
Prolonging the play unnecessarily.

It is a breach of the Proprieties to:

Use different designations for the same call ("A
Club," "I'll bid a club," etc., are incorrect. "One
club" is the only proper form).

Indicate any approval or disapproval of a call or play.

Indicate the expectation or intention of winning or
losing a trick before play to that trick has been
completed.

Comment or act during the auction or play to call
attention to a significant incident thereof, or to the
state of the score, or to the number of tricks that
will be required for success.

Look intently at any other player during the auction or
play, or at another player's hand for the purpose of
seeing his cards or observing the place from which
he draws a card.

Vary the normal tempo of bidding or play for the
purpose of disconcerting the other players.

COMMUNICATIONS BETWEEN PARTNERS:

Communication between partners during the auction and play
should be effected only by means of the calls and plays
themselves. Calls should be made in a uniform tone without
special emphasis or inflection, and without undue haste or
hesitation. Plays should be made without emphasis, gesture or
mannerism, and so far as possible, at a uniform rate.

It is improper for communication between partners to be effected through the *manner* in which calls and plays are made,
through extraneous remarks or gestures, or through questions
asked of the opponents or explanations given to them. When
a player has available to him improper information from his
partner's remark, question, explanation, gesture, mannerism,
special emphasis, inflection, haste or hesitation, *he should*

carefully avoid taking any advantage that might accrue to his side.

It is improper to have special understandings with partner regarding your bids and plays of which the opponents are unaware. The opponents are entitled to know about that fancy new bidding convention you and partner had decided to try out, and you are obliged to announce it to them before the game starts.

A NOTE ON PARTNERSHIP RAPPORT:

There are many bridge players who look on partner as a necessary evil, but your success at the bridge table will depend in great part on how well your partner performs. *Everything* that happens within your partnership can affect what kind of results you get, so your partner's morale should be important to you.

Nobody likes harsh criticism under any circumstances, but for people who play bridge seriously, the game is a real ego trip. We are sensitive about our game and our mistakes. If you point out your partner's errors right at the table (or, worse, if you are downright abusive), you won't accomplish anything constructive. On the contrary, you will probably get partner to dwell on his errors and induce him to play even worse.

A partnership at bridge is two people trying to act as one in an emotionally-charged setting. Recognize that when one player criticizes his partner, it is because he views partner's error as a direct reflection on his own ability; his ego has been ruffled.

You should always assume that your partner wants to win as badly as you do, and he is trying as hard as he can. Therefore, withold any criticism until after the game. Instead, you should be interested in *building* up his ego. If he makes an error, tell him that you would probably have done the same thing under the circumstances; or that he surely had what he thought was a good reason at the time he made his misguided bid or play.

126

Give his ego a chance to recover and he will play harder for the rest of the game.

Do your partner, your partnership and yourself a favor. Apply the Golden Rule when your partner makes an error.

AVOID CRITICIZING YOUR PARTNER.

Andersen THE LEBENSOHL CONVENTION COMPLETE .... $ 6.95
Baron THE BRIDGE PLAYER'S DICTIONARY $19.95
Bergen BETTER BIDDING WITH BERGEN,
    Vol. I, Uncontested Auctions $11.95
Bergen BETTER BIDDING WITH BERGEN,
    Vol. II, Competitive Auctions .... $ 9.95
Blackwood COMPLETE BOOK OF OPENING LEADS $17.95
Boeder THINKING ABOUT IMPS $12.95
Bruno-Hardy 2 OVER 1 GAME FORCE: AN INTRODUCTION .... $ 9.95
Darvas & De V. Hart RIGHT THROUGH THE PACK $14.95
Groner DUPLICATE BRIDGE DIRECTION $14.95
Hardy
    TWO-OVER-ONE GAME FORCE $14.95
    TWO-OVER-ONE GAME FORCE QUIZ BOOK $11.95
Harris BRIDGE DIRECTOR'S COMPANION (3rd Edition) $19.95
Kay COMPLETE BOOK OF DUPLICATE BRIDGE $14.95
Kearse BRIDGE CONVENTIONS COMPLETE $29.95
Kelsey THE TRICKY GAME $11.95
Lampert THE FUN WAY TO ADVANCED BRIDGE $11.95
Lawrence
    CARD COMBINATIONS $12.95
    COMPLETE BOOK ON BALANCING $11.95
    COMPLETE BOOK ON OVERCALLS $11.95
    DYNAMIC DEFENSE $11.95
    FALSECARDS .... $ 9.95
    HAND EVALUATION $11.95
    HOW TO READ YOUR OPPONENTS' CARDS $11.95
    JUDGMENT AT BRIDGE .... $ 9.95
    PARTNERSHIP UNDERSTANDINGS .... $ 4.95
    PLAY BRIDGE WITH MIKE LAWRENCE $11.95
    PLAY SWISS TEAMS WITH MIKE LAWRENCE .... $ 9.95
    WORKBOOK ON THE TWO OVER ONE SYSTEM $11.95
Lawrence & Hanson WINNING BRIDGE INTANGIBLES .... $ 4.95
Lipkin INVITATION TO ANNIHILATION .... $ 8.95
Michaels & Cohen 4-3-2-1 MANUAL .... $ 4.95
Penick BEGINNING BRIDGE COMPLETE .... $ 9.95
Penick BEGINNING BRIDGE QUIZZES .... $ 6.95
Reese & Hoffman PLAY IT AGAIN, SAM .... $ 7.95
Rosenkranz
    BRIDGE: THE BIDDER'S GAME $12.95
    TIPS FOR TOPS .... $ 9.95
    MORE TIPS FOR TOPS .... $ 9.95
    TRUMP LEADS .... $ 7.95
    OUR MAN GODFREY $10.95
Rosenkranz & Alder BID TO WIN, PLAY FOR PLEASURE $11.95
Rosenkranz & Truscott BIDDING ON TARGET $10.95
Simon
    WHY YOU LOSE AT BRIDGE $11.95
Stewart & Baron
    THE BRIDGE BOOK, Vol. 1, Beginning .... $ 9.95
    THE BRIDGE BOOK, Vol. 2, Intermediate .... $ 9.95
    THE BRIDGE BOOK, Vol. 3, Advanced .... $ 9.95
    THE BRIDGE BOOK, Vol. 4, Defense .... $ 7.95
Thomas SHERLOCK HOLMES, BRIDGE DETECTIVE .... $ 9.95
Woolsey
    MATCHPOINTS $14.95
    MODERN DEFENSIVE SIGNALLING .... $ 4.95
    PARTNERSHIP DEFENSE $12.95
World Bridge Federation APPEALS COMMITTEE DECISIONS
    from the 1994 NEC WORLD CHAMPIONSHIPS .... $ 9.95